osbkm

W9-DHV-836

I Think You're Wrong
(But I'm Listening)

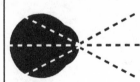

This Large Print Book carries the
Seal of Approval of N.A.V.H.

I THINK YOU'RE WRONG (BUT I'M LISTENING)

A GUIDE TO GRACE-FILLED POLITICAL CONVERSATIONS

SARAH STEWART HOLLAND AND BETH SILVERS

THORNDIKE PRESS
A part of Gale, a Cengage Company

Farmington Hills, Mich • San Francisco • New York • Waterville, Maine
Meriden, Conn • Mason, Ohio • Chicago

Copyright © 2019 by Sarah Stewart Holland and Beth Silvers.
Unless otherwise noted, Scripture quotations are taken from the Holy Bible, New International Version®, NIV®. Copyright © 1973, 1978, 1984, 2011 by Biblica, Inc.® Used by permission of Zondervan. All rights reserved worldwide. www.Zondervan.com. The "NIV" and "New International Version" are trademarks registered in the United States Patent and Trademark Office by Biblica, Inc.®
Scripture quotations marked AMP are from the Amplified® Bible, copyright © 1954, 1958, 1962, 1964, 1965, 1987 by The Lockman Foundation. Used by permission. (www.Lockman.org)
Thorndike Press, a part of Gale, a Cengage Company.

ALL RIGHTS RESERVED
Thorndike Press® Large Print Lifestyles.
The text of this Large Print edition is unabridged.
Other aspects of the book may vary from the original edition.
Set in 16 pt. Plantin.

LIBRARY OF CONGRESS CIP DATA ON FILE.
CATALOGUING IN PUBLICATION FOR THIS BOOK
IS AVAILABLE FROM THE LIBRARY OF CONGRESS

ISBN-13: 978-1-4328-6640-2 (hardcover alk. paper)

Published in 2019 by arrangement with Thomas Nelson, Inc., a division of HarperCollins Christian Publishing, Inc.

Printed in Mexico
1 2 3 4 5 6 7 23 22 21 20 19

To our children and our listeners,
who teach us grace every day.

Though we cannot think alike, may we not love alike? May we not be of one heart, though we are not of one opinion? Without all doubt, we may. Herein all the children of God may unite, notwithstanding these smaller differences.

— JOHN WESLEY,
SERMON 39 FROM CATHOLIC SPIRIT

CONTENTS

INTRODUCTION 11

PART ONE: START WITH YOU
Chapter 1: We Should Talk Politics . . 21
Chapter 2: Take Off Your Jersey. . . . 49
Chapter 3: Find Your Why 92
Chapter 4: Put Politics in Its Place . . 124

PART TWO: TURN YOUR EYES OUTWARD
Chapter 5: Give Grace. 149
Chapter 6: Get Curious 170
Chapter 7: Embrace the Paradox. . . 190
Chapter 8: Get Comfortable with
     Being Uncomfortable 213
Chapter 9: Exit the Echo Chamber. . 251
Chapter 10: Keep It Nuanced. . . . 275

ACKNOWLEDGMENTS 297
NOTES. 301
ABOUT THE AUTHORS 321

INTRODUCTION

Over the past few years, conversations about politics have started feeling toxic and hopeless. People we sit in the pew with every Sunday have begun to feel like strangers, and loved ones sitting across our dinner tables feel like enemies. When the news becomes sensational, we know that our Facebook feeds will turn from sweet baby videos and sunny vacation snapshots to ugly memes and hate-filled rants. Folks we witness every day as loving and kind suddenly feel vengeful and angry when discussing presidential candidates. A person who you know would give you the shirt off their back becomes just as likely to tell you that you're what's wrong with America if you talk about a controversial headline.

It's exhausting, and it's too much. Most of us know the issues are important, and we care about our communities and our countries. But we can't stand to fight with those

11

we love or argue with those we barely know. We feel spiritually dehydrated as we reel from the latest headlines and try to separate fact from fiction, so we've just decided it's best to tune it all out. But is it really? The two of us, perhaps like you, want to be part of a solution rather than accepting the current state of our politics as inevitable. This book is our attempt to "put on a heart of compassion, kindness, humility, gentleness, and patience," as Colossians 3:12 AMP advises, and find another way.

Whether you believe our country's problem is generational, geographical, or partisan, the most important thing to know about the polarization in American politics today is that we are choosing it. We are choosing division. We are choosing conflict. We are choosing to turn our civic sphere into a circus. We are choosing all of this, and we can choose otherwise.

Politics does not have to be driven by conflict and anger. We don't have to double down on our limited perceptions. We aren't destined to fall for the siren songs of righteousness ringing in our own ears. We can eschew cynicism and engage in thoughtful debate. We can put away extreme arguments and nasty rebuttals and bring the same care and respect to policy discussions that we bring to the rest of our lives.

Simply stated, there is a better way.

There is a way to engage with respect and empathy. There is a way to give grace and be vulnerable when discussing the issues that affect your family, your church, and your country. There is a way to stop treating politics like a team sport and get to work solving the real problems that plague our world. There is a way to talk about politics that leaves you inspired instead of depleted. There is a way to engage with each other that could (as it has in the distant past) lead to consensus and solutions, innovation and improvement. We, Sarah and Beth, know these things are true — because we try to live them.

Usually political books are written by professional pundits, journalists, and historians. That is not this book. We are approaching the conversation as wives, mothers, recovering attorneys, and women of faith. Before we started talking politics together, we knew each other primarily from our days as sorority sisters at Transylvania University and through a few shared motherhood moments on Facebook. Sarah knew Beth was a Republican, and Beth knew Sarah was a Democrat. (Because we all know Facebook isn't where we share *only* baby pics.) Eventually, Beth learned Sarah had been writing openly about politics on her parenting blog, and she started chiming in with comments and thoughts. Although we knew the labels of Democrat or Republican were where most conversations about politics began and ended in America, we wanted better, and through our small beginning conversations we recognized that was possible. We realized we wanted to model sane political conversations that prioritize relationships over point-scoring, mainly for ourselves and for our kids.

So, in November 2015, we started our podcast, *Pantsuit Politics.* We committed to having no agenda except to be real. No worrying that our moms or coworkers or clients would be listening. No filtering for our husbands or friends or pastors. We just wanted to openly discuss hard issues. We wanted to have the conversations that we couldn't find anywhere in the media. And we realized that having calm, kind conversations from opposing perspectives is more than possible — it is a spiritual imperative.

When we started talking, we felt exhausted and demoralized by the toxic environment surrounding politics. Now we relish the opportunity to hear each other's thoughts, to test our own beliefs against each other's philosophies, to strengthen our relationship by listening in order to understand, and to better appreciate our own core beliefs by having to articulate and challenge those beliefs.

This book discusses what we've learned and continue to learn from this practice. From hundreds of hours speaking to each other without an agenda other than to learn more about each other, ourselves, and the world, we've found a model for moving our country forward. If you're interested in journalism, a historical or academic perspective on particular moments in time, or professional political analysis, there are countless other resources that might be a better fit for you. But if you're interested in engaging with family and friends (even on Facebook!) about the issues of our time without feeling frustrated, angry, or hurt, then you've come to the right place. And if you're interested in leaving your political and media bubbles and getting curious about "the other side," then we've got strategies to get you started. We want this book to be a virtual kitchen table. If you want a fresh perspective on changing the country by changing our behaviors and holding a calm discussion in the midst of angry times, pull up a chair.

This book is divided into two sections. The first section acknowledges a hard spiritual truth we all learn over and over as people of faith: any problem, political or otherwise, starts with us. Blaming or, worse, trying to control others is never the solution. We have to thoroughly and critically examine our beliefs and values, and we have to face our weaknesses, mistakes, and limitations with humility and grace. Political conversation is a spiritual exercise in self-awareness, growth, and loving our neighbors if we are willing to be honest about our priorities, motivations, emotions, and behaviors.

Once we've done that, the second section encourages us to "turn our eyes outward" so that we reconnect as neighbors. We're not looking for agreement on every policy. We are looking for shared purpose, principles, and values. We are prioritizing our relationships as fellow citizens and children of God over our disagreements about specific legislation or representatives. We are bringing the principles we value in our faith and our lives — understanding, curiosity, and, above all, grace — to our civic engagement.

In each chapter we discuss one principle that we've learned for engaging with each other across the aisle. We bring in stories from our lives, from the news, and from history. Our families and our faith are part of these discussions. We realized early in the podcast that every experience we've had, lesson we've learned, and idea we've considered factors into how we engage in political discussions. Being transparent about what informs us as individuals leads us to more openhearted and productive conversations. We are both Christians (and we both have had ups and downs in our journeys). We didn't set out to talk about faith, but we quickly realized that you can't meaningfully discuss politics without getting clear on your values. For us, that means incorporating our faith. We do not intend for that faith to be exclusive. Fundamental to both of our belief systems is that we are all one. Whatever you do or do not believe in, this book is for you, and we hope our explorations of our values help you find new ways to examine and articulate the principles that guide your political participation.

Throughout this book, know that we see you as a respected guest in our homes as we discuss our ideas. At the end of each chapter, we share a reflection exercise to invite you to keep the discussion going. Our goal with every podcast we create, every speech we give, and every paragraph we write is to start a conversation. If it ends with us, we haven't fulfilled our purpose. Some of these exercises will speak to you more than others, and that's okay. Many times, you'll probably disagree with us. That's okay too. This table, like our country, is at its best when it is a big, messy collaboration. We hope that you'll want to stay at our virtual kitchen table and then take these conversations into your homes and pews and maybe even your Facebook feeds, because we believe politics can be a source of connection even when we disagree. Most importantly, we hope that you'll feel that you belong at this table. Our country, our communities, our churches, and our city halls need your voice and perspective.

We're honored that you're here. We know American politics is ugly right now and that it's tempting to avoid the arena. We can choose otherwise. Let's do it together.

■ ■ ■ ■

Part One:
Start with You

■ ■ ■ ■

Chapter One:
We Should Talk Politics

We all know the rule. The rule governs church functions, social outings, and family gatherings. The rule is passed down through generations and tended to with particular care by women. The rule is for our own good. The rule prevents fights and conflicts and all appearances of discomfort.

The rule is simple: don't talk politics or religion.

It's rude. It's tacky. It's unladylike. It will ruin Thanksgiving, ensure your first time teaching Sunday school is your last, quickly end a first date, maybe cost you a promotion. We were both taught at a young age that mentioning anything political is not appropriate in polite conversation, especially for women. The phrase "not to get political" is embedded in our vocabularies and jumps out of our mouths almost reflexively. At family dinners, our grandmothers discouraged any discussion of the latest political scandal or presidential outrage, glossing over uncomfortable moments by ushering everyone toward dessert. Over many years of Sunday suppers, holiday parties, and family reunions, we learned that women shouldn't make people uncomfortable, especially with their opinions about politics.

It hasn't always been this way, and it doesn't have to stay this way. There is a way out of this click-baiting, hyperpolarized, road-to-nowhere cycle. We just have to learn to talk to each other again.

History shows that we have the capacity for problem-solving, even through vigorous disagreement. Our founding fathers and mothers believed in talking politics. Many historians cite the desire to assemble and debate as central to America itself. Hannah Arendt, in *On Revolution,* argued "that the people went to the town assemblies, as their representatives later were to go to the famous Conventions, neither exclusively because of duty nor, and even less, to serve their own interests but most of all because *they enjoyed the discussions, the delibera-tions, and the making of decisions.*"[1]

They *enjoyed* it.

Somewhere along the way, we lost our revolutionary passion for talking about the issues that affect our country and our lives.

We decided that conversational conflict is impolite at best and dangerous at worst. Unfortunately our attempts to avoid these uncomfortable moments have backfired. In our efforts to protect relationships from political tension, we have instead escalated that tension. Because the reality is that we never stopped talking politics altogether — we stopped talking politics with people who disagree with us. We changed "you shouldn't talk about politics" to "you should talk only to people who reinforce your worldview." Instead of giving ourselves the opportunity to be molded and informed and tested by others' opinions, we allowed our opinions and our hearts to harden.

We sorted ourselves, engaging only with those who were on *our* side. We also sorted others — based solely on assumptions about *their* hardened opinions. In the process, we subconsciously and constantly increased the stakes in believing that our personal perspectives are accurate and morally superior.

Today, if and when we do enter a discussion with someone from the other side, we're ready for battle, not dialogue. The rule that was supposed to prevent others' discomfort has become a weapon to protect us from our own. Somehow, a concern about others' feelings has morphed into an obsession with clinging to our talking points, as though those talking points form the very basis of who we are and what we stand for. We don't want to be challenged or even questioned, because we believe there is too much at stake. We have tied together our religious beliefs, our pride in our upbringings, and our policy positions until they've become like a tangled mess of necklaces that we shove in a drawer — still treasured but unwearable. And over time we have lost the ability to sort out why we believe what we believe about our neighbors and perhaps even about ourselves. Approval ratings for politicians in both parties have bottomed out, and our faith in public and private institutions is at an all-time low. It's no wonder that protests turn violent so regularly that we hardly notice. These were once the spaces — from political parties to pews to protests — where we worked out our disagreements, or at least got comfortable hearing opposing opinions. We've stopped practicing good conversations. We've disconnected from one another.

If the ramifications of political conversation ended at even the most contentious dinner table, or if these uncomfortable situations were simply a cable television drama that we could turn off, our instincts to confirm our beliefs and avoid any conversations that challenge them wouldn't be so dangerous. Perhaps we *could* continue on the path of tuning out the cacophony of political debate. But the reality is that we cannot opt out of the real consequences of politics in our lives. Politics becomes policy, and policy is the road map for the more than five hundred thousand elected officials who make decisions every single day — decisions that determine the roads we drive on, the schools our children attend, the wars we wage, and the taxes we pay. When we struggle at all levels to get anything done — to pass budgets, confirm judicial nominees, and perform even the most basic functions of government, like ensuring our water is safe to drink — it is our daily lives that are affected. This dysfunction isn't what we want for our children, and it shouldn't be what we want for ourselves.

Regular people — parents and non-parents, people of faith and atheists, students and teachers, people of all backgrounds and cultures — have to discuss how we want our governments to function and what we want our country to become. We need people who are worried about gas prices and their 401(k)s and student-loan interest rates and laundry and day care to talk about domestic policy. We need people who remember the draft and the uncle who died in Afghanistan and the friend who missioned abroad in Spain to talk about foreign policy. We need parents of children with special needs and gifts talking about education policy. We need people who work help desks across the United States thinking about cybersecurity. We need to show up with the entirety of our life experiences for these conversations.

We need to bring our voices and perspectives to the table calmly, with respect for ourselves and one another, recognizing that we do not live alone. America has never been and will never be homogeneous. We are here to bump up against each other. We need to bring our faith and values not just to specific issues but to the process of engaging in civil discourse. We can share our perspectives on even the most controversial and personal topics. Doing so will de-escalate the rhetoric and open pathways for solutions, innovation, and a stronger national identity.

Others will disagree with us. We have to expect that. *Debate* is not a dirty word, even if you feel underinformed or ill prepared. It is easy to envision the famous paintings of the Constitutional Convention and think of our founding mothers and fathers as a monolithic group who always agreed. However, anyone who has sung along to Lin-Manuel Miranda's blockbuster Broadway musical *Hamilton* knows nothing could be further from the truth. Our patriotic ancestors battled it out over everything from war strategies to presidential pageantry. In fact, let us not forget that they got it plain wrong with the Articles of Confederation before they finally settled on the Constitution we now enshrine as infallible.

They didn't give up because it was hard, and neither should we. It is nothing short of our patriotic duty to engage with one another as Americans — and not only with those Americans who look like us and act like us and agree with us. We face difficult challenges as a country. We face problems that won't be solved in our lifetimes. That doesn't mean we shouldn't try. Throwing our hands up in frustration is a natural reaction to a problem as big as America's current political climate, but that's only because we feel so disconnected from America's greatest strength — each other.

Learning to have healthy conflict with each other over political challenges is of utmost importance; in fact, it is a spiritual imperative. We do not demonstrate love toward our neighbors by demonizing them over how they feel about tax policy or reproductive rights. We do not turn the other cheek when we treat politics as an insular sphere in which fighting fire with fire is the only way. We do not live as the hands and feet of a loving creator when we opt out of the processes that dictate roads and bridges, school curriculum and water treatment, war and peace. Neither stridence nor apathy is a virtue. Like it or not, the decisions our government both makes and does not make impact every aspect of our lives. Democratic societies, like churches, are a body. We all affect each other. We can't sit it out. We can't move forward if we refuse to ask each other where we want to go.

Talking politics not only has the power to make our communities, states, and country better, but it also has the power to make us better as individuals. Connecting with one another isn't just the source of American strength. It is also the source of faith, hope, love, and understanding. Our conversations help us to understand on a much deeper level many of the issues that tear America apart. Talking about subjects most people studiously avoid in mixed political company helps us to see where we are right, where we are wrong, and where we have more to learn. More than that, talking with one another helps us to better understand ourselves, to clarify our values and priorities, and to confront weaknesses and attitudes we could have too easily ignored.

And here's the most surprising thing the two of us have found in talking for a few hours each week about everything from trade policy to the role of the Supreme Court: we enjoy it. Our grannies' hearts may have been in the right place with all their shushing, but we'd rather channel our inner Abigail Adams than take a second helping of pie. Adams said, "If we mean to have Heroes, Statesmen and Philosophers, we should have learned women,"[2] and that's what we intend to help each other become. Engaging in the issues of our time with people we love, or simply people who love this country as much as we do, is fun. That doesn't mean it's easy. It isn't. But in the immortal words of Jimmy Dugan in *A League of Their Own,* "It's supposed to be hard. If it wasn't hard, everyone would do it. The hard is what makes it great."[3]

So let's do the hard but enjoyable work begun by our founding fathers and mothers. Let's talk politics.

In very different ways, the two of us have

been talking politics our whole lives.

Sarah learned to talk early and never really stopped, especially as an only child encouraged by the doting adults in her life. When she was young, she thought she had a love of the stage and should pursue acting. Eventually she realized it wasn't the stage that she loved — it was the microphone. She had plenty of opinions, especially about politics, ready to share. To exactly no one's surprise she was named Most Talkative in high school. Of course, a young woman with passionate political opinions wasn't always well received. Sarah spent most of her childhood battling peers (and some adults) who constantly told her to tone it down if she wanted to be liked. Still, with the dream of one day running for office always in the back of her mind, she majored in political science and attended law school in Washington, DC. After graduation she began working in politics, first for Hillary Clinton's 2007 presidential campaign and then as a legislative aide in the United States Senate.

However, Sarah's political pursuits took a major detour in 2009 when she convinced her husband, Nicholas, to move to her hometown of Paducah, Kentucky, before the birth of their first son. She rebuilt her life as a stay-at-home mom to (eventually) three boys and as a mommy blogger. By 2015 she had just begun to tiptoe back into the political arena and had recently graduated from Emerge Kentucky, a training program for Democratic women considering public office. Her husband, a passionate podcast listener, kept pestering her to start a podcast.

Sarah had always loved talking politics, but she was no longer a Capitol Hill staffer or even a practicing lawyer. Who would care what she had to say? She was interested in how women worked in the political arena, and she knew that topic would increase in importance with what seemed like the inevitable candidacy of Hillary Clinton in 2016. So Sarah thought she might start interviewing women in politics. She did a few interviews, found them a little boring, and, never one to do something if she was only in it half-heartedly, did nothing with the files for months.

Talking politics by herself was simply too scary.

Enter Beth.

Or reenter. We first met our freshman year of college at Transylvania University. Just as we do now, we had very different approaches to life then, and despite being in the same sorority, our paths were more parallel than intertwined. By 2015 we were close enough to be friends on Facebook — brought together again by our similar journeys toward natural birth (a story for another chapter). Beth had reached out for advice several times, knowing that Sarah had had two successful home births, and they struck up a casual friendship that eventually led to Beth writing guest posts for Sarah's blog while Beth was on maternity leave.

In the summer of 2015, Beth wrote a guest post with a one-word title. That one word would become the clarion call of our podcast and an underlying theme of this book: *nuance.*

In a reaction to the ever-increasing Facebook vitriol, she suggested a simple hashtag of #nuance to signal the acknowledgment of the complexity behind issues. Complexity that doesn't always fit in a status update. She wrote:

This summer, the internet appears to have caught a case of False Dichotomy-tosis. With every opinion on a major news story comes a flurry of memes, charts, and comments announcing that that's YOUR WRONG OPINION and this is MY RIGHT ASSERTION OF REALITY and our positions on this topic are mutually exclusive.

It seems we need a way to acknowledge that the limited characters in our social media discourse don't always afford space for a complete expression of thought.

I hate to diagnose a problem without offering a cure, so here's my proposal: if you're posting about current events or other controversial topics (or topics that you can't believe are controversial-but-trust-me-they-will-be-when-you-expose-them-to-the-scrutiny-of-your-Facebook-friends), just end the post with #Nuance as sort of a modern footnote, telling the reader, "I have more to say but I'm out of time, and you're out of interest. Please don't make a bunch of weird assumptions based on this post, cool?" I understand that the world really doesn't need another hashtag, but it seems from scrolling my feeds that we need a short way to introduce some fine print on our tweets and status updates. . . .

Here's the thing: we don't have to stake out extremes, and doing so is reductive and unworthy of our democracy. Our social media discourse matters, so we should elevate it by asking questions, fleshing out ideas, and respectfully engaging with each other. If we can't or won't do those things, we can at least stop assuming that someone is against everything we believe in based on a single tweet. You can believe in gun control and care about the Second Amendment. You can acknowledge the existence of man-made climate change and God (for that matter, you can even acknowledge global warming on a snowy day). You can be against drug use and pro-legalization. You can pray every night and believe prayer in school is problematic. We can and should examine our positions and allow for depth in both our own perspectives and the perspectives of others. Go forth and tweet, Facebook, and blog — just make space for the entirety of the conversation.[4]

The reaction to the post across both of our social media channels was a resounding *amen*! Sarah immediately realized that one more interview show wasn't what the world needed.

The world needed nuance.

Sarah suggested to Beth that they start a podcast. Beth said yes, and we decided to start talking politics.

Or, at least in retrospect, it seems that simple. In reality, Beth had serious trepidation. While Sarah had spent a lifetime being told she was unlikable because she shared her opinions, Beth had built a successful career on being likable and learning to keep her opinions to herself in the process. Raised on a small dairy farm in western Kentucky, Beth was always the star student and rewarded leader. Until very recently, a wall in her childhood home was covered with her trophies, plaques, and ribbons. These awards, as well as the leadership roles she was asked to take in college, taught her one thing: women are rewarded for doing what is expected of them and making everyone around them feel good in the process.

We were once asked by Matt Marr on his podcast, *The Dear Mattie Show,* what the title of our memoirs would be. Beth answered without hesitation, *"Beige Wallpaper."*[5] She had gone to law school because it was expected of her and had taken a high-paying law firm job afterward because, how could she say no? She had been taught, over and over, that when you have the ability to do something, you always have the responsibility to do it. But she was never happy. She tried different practice areas, bouncing from domestic relations to general litigation to corporate bankruptcy work, where she stuck it out for almost five years. After her first daughter was born, she used the skills built over a lifetime of making people comfortable to try a career in human resources.

She pitched her firm on a human resources position and got herself hired for it. She would go on to become the firm's chief people officer. But she was still miserable. Beth was a walking complaint department, a workplace therapist, and a sounding board. She tried reinventing her position, but she couldn't find the right fit. Something was missing in her life. She worried that the only fitting epitaph on her gravestone would say, "We didn't know her, but she made us feel good."

So how does a woman trained to make people comfortable begin doing the exact thing that makes so many of us uncomfortable? How does she talk politics? How does she talk politics *as a woman,* as a people-pleaser, and as someone who typically became whatever she needed to become based on the situation?

We sat down to our microphones with those questions and so many more in our ears, Beth on the floor in her closet surrounded by her corporate wardrobe and Sarah barricaded in her bedroom still filled with baby gear from her third son born earlier that year. We struggled with getting the volume right in our recordings, because Sarah tended to speak loudly and soulfully while Beth's self-described "Delicious Dish" voice barely registered on the microphone. Sarah was fiery and excited, which led her to interrupt Beth often. Beth, always editing herself and trying to balance her perspective with Sarah's, needed painfully long pauses after Sarah spoke to collect her thoughts.

We did as much research and preparation as we could while juggling our families and careers. When we started the podcast, Sarah had three boys: six-year-old Griffin, four-year-old Amos, and nine-month-old Felix. Beth had two girls: newborn Ellen and four-year-old Jane. We recorded before work and after putting the kids in bed. Sarah worried that no one would care what she had to say, that she might not really know what she was talking about, or that she could say something that would make someone angry or hurt their feelings. Beth worried that people would listen and realize how little they knew about her. More than that, she worried about how little she knew about herself. But we talked like two old friends reconnecting and creating a hobby that felt like something between a college elective and therapy.

Since our less than auspicious beginnings, we have realized that being women talking about politics isn't a liability; it's an asset. For far too long, the voices of women — particularly in the media — have been largely excluded. While many women journalists have been doing thorough and expert reporting for decades, rarely have women shown up to share their opinions. The fact that we can all easily list well-known women pundits on two hands is indicative of the problem, not representative of any positive movement for change. Men dominate politics. But we discovered almost immediately after starting our podcast that both women *and men* desperately want to hear another perspective.

Despite a saturated political media market, the two of us couldn't find the kind of political conversations we were looking for. So we decided to have those conversations ourselves. Together, we brought to the discussion a host of experiences that were not usually represented. We were both daughters in families that had aging grandparents and parents, so we understood the caregiving roles that many adults had to play. We were mothers to small children, so issues of childcare, public education, and reproductive health had real-life consequences in our daily lives. Our professional experiences encompassed working outside the home full time during motherhood, maintaining a full-time focus on raising children, and pursuing entrepreneurship. Our families were laboratories for the future of work and the ever-changing economy.

We started to see that these everyday experiences we brought to the table as women didn't disqualify us, but rather made us different kinds of experts. We weren't sociologists, scientists, or researchers. Neither were we professional journalists, government bureaucrats, or pundits. We were just two women outside the Beltway admitting their biases and confusion and emotions around issues. This struck a chord with others out there just like us who were hungry for an honest dialogue that was grounded in context and values rather than drama and a false sense of neutrality.

We worked on presenting background information to the best of our abilities, never assuming our listeners were foreign-policy experts or lawyers or even particularly knowledgeable about politics. We also tried to avoid condescension and to treat our listeners with respect. We wanted the complexity, and we assumed our listeners did too. We acknowledged our partisan leanings at the beginning of every show by introducing ourselves as "Sarah from the Left" and

"Beth from the Right." We did not do this because we wanted to frame our conversations as equal showdowns between two sides. Instead we wanted to acknowledge our worldviews, so we could get to the more important work of figuring out the realities of the issues we were discussing and the possibilities for moving forward.

We also made a commitment to be vulnerable and honest. We tried not to edit ourselves, and to verbally acknowledge when we were feeling angry, frustrated, or attacked. We did not see ourselves as representatives of the Democratic Party or GOP and therefore did not feel any obligation to stick to the party talking points. If we were disappointed in our party leaders, we said so. There were no outside influences pulling the strings. Our producers were our husbands, who did our sound engineering (and complained about our tendency to say "um"), and listeners who financially contributed to the podcast. So we felt the freedom to decide what to cover, when and how to cover it, and to talk in depth about events in our own lives that have informed our opinions on issues.

If we ever worried that what we said could be misinterpreted, we expressed that fear and said it anyway. And we found that our listeners — through emails and comments on social media — responded with the same amount of honesty and vulnerability.

It's been interesting to see the reactions to our conversations. Some people are confused. When they hear that one of us is liberal and one is conservative, they expect a debate format. And why wouldn't they? Partisan sparring is the only form of discussion making its way to our televisions, radios, and feeds. Anytime we receive feedback that we should disagree more often, we talk with our listeners openly about that feedback. There are two molds our podcast could fit into, and both of those molds would probably be easier (and almost certainly more profitable) than what we're doing today: we could be a combative debate show, or we could pick one "side" and be yet another place where listeners validate their worldviews. But molds are for Jell-O, not people.

We didn't want that for ourselves, and we don't want that for you either. In every discussion, we recommit to our promise: "No shouting, no insults, plenty of nuance."

We share the backstory of our podcast because we want you to know that if we can have these conversations, so can you. We want you to know that what we see on television and hear on the radio doesn't have to be the blueprint for talking with our friends and neighbors and fellow church members. What creates clicks online or sells ads during prime time doesn't have to drive the conversations in our living rooms. We can do better.

By talking politics honestly and earnestly as yourself — not as a representative of the party to which you happen to be registered or as a polite foil for the person in your life who is more impassioned about politics than you are — you add your unique experiences and opinions and perspective to a space that needs you. You also sign up to be vulnerable, to be challenged, and to evolve.

You know how some people seem to freeze at a point in time? They decide they don't want to learn another new technology. They're happy with their hair, and they've found the perfect brand of jeans that they're staying with. The music from their high school days makes them happy, so that's all they listen to. Curiously and charmingly, these folks become like wax statues for particular eras. There's nothing wrong with that, but it's not what we want for our brains, especially when the world is changing faster all the time.

The righteousness of unchallenged thought freezes us in time. We double and triple down on opinions even as some of the information that we're basing those opinions on changes. We cling to views even when those views are based on experiences that are divorced from the present and future. The world changes; we need to be vigilant about what stands the test of time and what needs to change with it. If you never engage with the world, the world — full of people you love and people who get on your nerves — never has a chance to push and pull you in new directions.

As we'll discuss at length throughout this book, this doesn't mean changing the essential character of who you are or abandoning your most deeply held principles. There are core principles that shouldn't be compromised, and, as we mentioned earlier, the perspective you bring, shaped by who you are and what you stand behind, is irreplaceable. We aren't asking you to throw out your values and beliefs, abandon your upbringing, or turn your back on the people and groups that are important to you. We also aren't asking you to agree with either of us or anyone else. Our prevailing philosophy is "you do you" — be who you were made to be, make your own decisions, and live your best life. We just want you to actually do *you* — not Rachel Maddow or Sean Hannity — based on the experiences that you're having every day and the values that you want to infuse into your life. And we want you to do you with your friends and neighbors and fellow parishioners and colleagues. Political pundits have become fond of discussing partisan politics as "tribal." We don't want your tribe to be your political party. We want it to be the communities in which you live, worship, and work — diverse in thought as they may be.

Engaging with other people is never easy, but it is always worth it. Engaging with other people about politics is no different. Let yourself take that chance. Let yourself rise to the challenge. Your ability to stretch and grow will surprise you, and so will the people around you. Once people see you as a person willing to have thoughtful, curious, calm discussions, you will have all kinds of interesting conversations that seemed impossible a year ago. People you thought you understood will leave you slack jawed in awe of their empathy and compassion. People you thought were kind listeners will surprise you with their passionate and previously unshared thoughts on policy. You'll have new appreciation for the people around you, new ideas about how to solve problems in your own life and in the public sphere, and perhaps new inspiration about your place in the tapestry of our democracy.

Talking politics is a gift to yourself and to the world. Ultimately, politics is really about people. People are never boring, and people belong together. We are meant to hash out how we want to live in community with one another. We're meant to sort out our different beliefs about what government should and shouldn't do, what laws and programs we do and don't need, and how we should and shouldn't spend taxpayer dollars.

Our description might sound far-fetched given the pitch of political conversations today. Some prep work is essential for the shift in conversation that we're describing. Over the next several chapters, we're going to talk about questions you need to ask yourself before you are ready to open the door to engaging with other people. Then, in part 2, we'll share our specific thoughts about having better dialogue on contentious topics. By the end of this book, we hope that you'll find, as the two of us have, that continuous engagement in political conversation from a place of loving-kindness is a deeply enriching practice.

CONTINUE THE CONVERSATION

Sarah loves exercises and checklists that help her track her progress. She loves a good bullet journal, app, or program to assure her that she's engaged in an effort that will make a difference. Beth was a top student as a child and is a workaholic as an adult. Given our personalities, it seems only fitting that we end each chapter with some homework! More than that, we want to make sure that we're sharing ideas that serve as catalysts for your thinking and action. So, we are closing with questions and thoughts that we hope help you further explore and apply the chapter's theme in your life. And because our faith so influences our thoughts, we're leaving for those of like mind a passage of scripture that they might find applicable.

1. Have you been given the message that you shouldn't talk about politics or religion? If you have, what effect has it had on you? Do you think that being a man or woman influenced the messages you received?
2. When was the last time you engaged in a political conversation with someone who disagreed with you? How did you leave that interaction feeling? How did

the conversation impact your relationship with that person?

3. Because you cannot have too much
Abigail Adams, here are some more
thoughts from her that we feel are
particularly relevant as we all begin to
engage in politics again:

> These are times in which a Genious
> would wish to live. It is not in the still
> calm of life, or the repose of a pacific
> station, that great characters are
> formed. . . . The Habits of a vigorous
> mind are formed in contending with dif-
> ficulties. . . . Great necessities call out
> great virtues. When a mind is raised,
> and animated by scenes that engage
> the Heart, then those qualities which
> would otherwise lay dormant, wake
> into Life, and form the Character of the
> Hero and the Statesman.[6]

How might this passage impact your
thoughts about discussing politics with
people with differing opinions?

4. Ephesians 4 tells us that "we are all
members of one body" and that we
should "not let the sun go down while
[we] are still angry" (vv. 25–26). The
chapter ends, "Be kind and compas-

sionate to one another, forgiving each other, just as in Christ God forgave you" (v. 32). Paul's instructions feel like important advice today. Consider how his words in this chapter counsel us to participate politically.

Chapter Two:
Take Off Your Jersey

You've seen the headlines.

> January 19, 2018 — *Business Insider* reported that a top Senate Republican "threw cold water" on a "Hail Mary plan" that would have averted a government shutdown.[1]

> March 20, 2013 — President Obama said that the use of chemical weapons by the Assad regime in Syria would be "a game changer."[2]

> December 2002 — CIA director George Tenet, in response to President George W. Bush's question about his level of certainty about the case for war in Iraq, said, "Don't worry, it's a slam dunk."[3]

The horse race. The front-runner. Knock-out punches. Putting points on the board. We constantly speak of politics in sports analogies. Despite not being ardent sports fans (except for Beth's love of Kentucky basketball), the two of us find ourselves slipping into sports parlance all the time when discussing politics, and you might too.

There's nothing wrong with "moving the ball down the field," "getting across the goal line," and otherwise bringing sports language into our discussions. But sometimes we take sports too far. From the stands, it's easy to show our children that we love them more when they win and a little less when they make an error. It's easy to forget our values when it's tied in the bottom of the ninth inning with runners in scoring position. It's easy to leave behind what we learned in Sunday school when the referee makes a bad call with thirty seconds left in the second half.

We take our sports too seriously because someone has to win and someone has to lose. That's why there is a big problem with behaving as though politics is a sport when we are focused on winning as a political imperative. Our civic participation should be about finding the best solutions possible under the circumstances, about trying to serve everyone who shares this country (and our states and municipalities). To dig ourselves out of a political winner-take-all mind-set, we have to explore the problem honestly and vulnerably.

For most people who are passionate about politics (though not everyone — we see you, Libertarians and Greens!), there are two teams: Democrats vs. Republicans, conservatives vs. liberals, right vs. left. Many of us are born into one of the two and are taught by our parents and community that only one party could possibly represent our values. Some of us reject our family's chosen team and join the other team with the zeal of the converted. Some of us stay put and would feel like a traitor if we dared consider voting differently. Either way, we put on our team jerseys and adopt the policies, positions, and politicians expected of us.

The parties are, for some of us, necessary shorthand. We're busy thinking about whether we filled out the field trip permission form, picked up the tomatoes we need to make chili for a potluck, or paid the credit card bill. When we're raising small children, working long hours, or trying to make ends meet while getting to every soccer game, it's hard to pay attention to the intricacies of our military policy in Afghanistan and the effects of a new banking regulation. Using the parties as shorthand is understandable, but using the parties as orthodoxy is dangerous. Many of us have crossed that line.

Very few of us examine our chosen team's ideas or scrutinize our team's candidates. The number of people who actually read each party's platforms, which lay out positions on everything from Social Security to Saudi Arabia, is unlikely to fill a tennis doubles team, much less a baseball dugout. Reporting tells us that even many members of Congress don't read the party platforms or the legislation they vote for. Even fewer of us are willing to disagree with the party line on particular issues. No, once we've put on the jersey, it acts as a blinder. We see only the team. Nothing else matters.

It doesn't matter if that policy makes us uncomfortable or if we don't even understand it. It doesn't matter if that position doesn't align with our values. It doesn't matter if that politician gives us the creeps. We are team players, and nothing comes before the team.

It's so easy to fall into the team sports mind-set. For many of us, the jerseys become our entire identity, informing everything from the articles we retweet to the types of music we enjoy. We recite the talking points and are unwilling to even entertain the idea that we could be wrong. We enter every conversation as an opportunity to score points for our team while simultaneously staying on the defensive. If a member of our team appears in the latest breaking-news bulletin, we're justifying their bad behavior before Wolf Blitzer can cut to the first commercial break by talking about how much worse those other guys are.

Beth grew up near Kentucky's border with Indiana and constantly heard mean spirited jokes traded between Wildcats and Hoosiers. She never really understood that aspect of athletic rivalry. Sadly, that same kind of identity-driven mean spiritedness has come to define the relationships between Democrats and Republicans.

Our jerseys not only blind us to ourselves, but also to the world around us. If we live our entire lives inside the arena, we never notice that aspects of the game we're playing may no longer be relevant. On so many topics, it seems the two sides are arguing about issues from perspectives that no longer exist. We debate welfare as the nature of work fundamentally changes. We debate urban versus rural lifestyles as technology fundamentally changes the way we live no matter our zip codes. We stay focused on the scoreboard, forgetting that time marches on outside the arena. Everything is seen through our identity as a team player, and we miss the spaces where so much more is going on than national debates.

Even in local races — like the nonpartisan one Sarah ran for in her hometown of Paducah — the team mentality colors voter perspectives and media coverage. Everything from city hall races to school board decisions become a field on which to play out our national political battles. Professor Steven Rogers of Saint Louis University studies the election of state representatives. He found that many voters could not name their representatives or what they stood for due in large part to an absence of media coverage on local political issues. In the absence of information, the state legislators were most directly affected by the popularity of the US president's party in their districts. Looking at polls from three different elections, Professor Rogers discovered that voters' attitudes toward the president were three times more important than their attitudes toward the state legislators themselves.[4] In other words, "If you're on the president's team and I don't like him, I'm not voting for you. If you're on his team and I do like him, then you must be fine too." This is true even though where our local officials stand on parks and libraries matters a lot more than where they stand on the corporate income tax rate or whether the government should subsidize ethanol.

When our jerseys inform everything, it stifles our creativity. Compromise is out of the question because only one side can win. There is no innovation. We evaluate ideas not by their merit, but by who proposed them. The rules of the game have been preordained, and we consent to those rules by wearing our jerseys. These "rules" weren't written or agreed to by any of us, but we act as though they inevitably inform our political participation. Anytime we try challenging the rules, someone is quick to point out that things don't work that way in the real world. But politics as defined by partisan bickering and fueled by petty punditry isn't the real world. It's the field, and beyond the field exists a space in which we have the agency to analyze problems and solutions independently.

The jersey also blinds us to the humanity of the other side. This team-sport mentality has created a toxic mix of competition and confirmation bias. Our team is *never* wrong, and the other team is *always* wrong. Somewhere along the way we stopped disagreeing with each other and started hating each other. We are enemies, and *our* side is engaged in an existential battle for the very soul of the country. We are no longer working toward common goals. We are no longer building something together. Our sole objective is tearing the other side down. Nothing short of total victory is acceptable. Again, it's much like how we view college basketball in Kentucky: We can't just beat the other side. We have to annihilate them.

Polls bear out this grim perspective. In 2017, the Pew Research Center conducted the largest political study in its history in an effort to understand polarization in American politics. Over the course of a year, they interviewed more than ten thousand Americans, and the results show that we are taking this team-sport mentality to increasingly hostile places. It's not just that we are escalating our affiliation to our own teams. Pew found heightened antipathy toward the other team as well. Twenty years ago, only 17 percent of Republicans had a "very unfavorable" opinion of Democrats. By 2016, almost half of all Republicans had a "very unfavorable view." A similar shift was seen on the other side. In twenty years, the number of Democrats who had "very unfavorable" opinions of Republicans jumped from 16 percent to 44 percent. Among those on both sides who had a "very unfavorable" opinion of the other party, the majority reported to Pew that the opposing party's policies represent a *threat* to the future of the country.[5]

This hardened response to those on the "other team" is not an invention of modern American politics. It seems to be hardwired into the circuitry of our brains. The Old Testament is filled with stories of sometimes deadly tribalism, and scientific data gives us insight into why that happens. In 1968, elementary school teacher Jane Elliott conducted a famous experiment with her students in the days after the assassination of Dr. Martin Luther King Jr. She divided the class by eye color. The brown-eyed children were told they were better. They were the "in-group." The blue-eyed children were told they were less than the brown-eyed children — hence becoming the "out-group." Suddenly, former classmates who had once played happily side by side were taunting and torturing one another on the playground. Lest we assign greater morality to the "out-group," the blue-eyed children were just as quick to attack the brown-eyed children once the roles were reversed.[6]

Since Elliott's experiment, researchers have conducted thousands of studies to understand the in-group/out-group response. Now, with fMRI scans, these researchers can actually see which parts of our brains fire up when perceiving a member of an out-group. In a phenomenon called the out-group homogeneity effect, we are more likely to see members of our groups as unique and individually motivated — and more likely to see a member of the out-group as the same as everyone else in that group. When we encounter this out-group member, our amygdala — the part of our brain that processes anger and fear — is more likely to become active. The more we perceive this person outside our group as a threat, the more willing we are to treat them badly.

Elliott's research helps us understand why we've started to talk about our fellow Americans as enemies of the nation simply for registering with a different party than ours. We've always sought out ways to sort ourselves. As our world shrinks and former ways of sorting ourselves become antiquated and clearly understood as harmful, we've homed in on political affiliation as a legitimate dividing line. Our elected officials have seized on this partisan polarization and believe the "team" is the top priority. Campaigns have become multimillion-dollar enterprises that approach elections the same way they might approach trying to influence our choices of soft drinks or shoes. They seek to make us brand loyal, and we're falling for it.

In 2016 major party presidential campaigns created thousands of Facebook ads a day, some micro-targeted to individual user preferences, down to the background colors and fonts. In debates, we ask candidates for a set of promises based on hypothetical scenarios and incomplete information — looking for nothing more than team loyalty in a million different expressions. "What will you do about the nuclear threat posed by North Korea?" a moderator asks one candidate who has never received a security briefing and another who cannot share everything she knows because it's classified. As voters, we act as though we don't want our candidates to go into office as people who will take in new information, learn, and adapt their views based on that learning. We want a commitment: a vote for tax cuts no matter the budget needs, or preservation of Social Security even if it becomes unsustainable. Support the team or else!

Some politicians explicitly express this mind-set. Former senator Rick Santorum stated it plainly several years ago when defending his support for the education legislation No Child Left Behind:

> I have to admit, I voted for that, it was against the principles I believed in, but you know, when you're part of the team, sometimes you take one for the team, for the leader, and I made a mistake. You know, politics is a team sport, folks, and sometimes you've got to rally together and do something, and in this case I thought testing and finding out how bad the problem was wasn't a bad idea.[7]

Regardless of whether other members of Congress are as forthcoming as Senator Santorum, the voting records show that all our legislators are acting in similar ways. In 2015 a group of academics studied the roll-call votes of the House of Representatives from 1949 to 2012. For decades, the researchers found what they call cross-party pairs: legislators from different parties that voted the same way. Beginning in the mid-1990s, the number of cross-party pairs greatly decreased, and today the pairs are almost nonexistent.[8]

Unfortunately, the game is never over. The season never comes to an end. At least in sports, the truest of fans can't live only in the stands. The timer expires. The season eventually wraps. There's an off-season for resting and recharging (and players are even traded! How's that for a mind-bending political metaphor?). But in politics the game never stops. Presidential races stretch on for years, and every new president fuels a new movement — be it the Tea Party or the Resistance — that turns every subsequent special election and midterm into the most important election *ever.* Most politicians never come out of campaign mode, logging hundreds of hours making fundraising calls even in nonelection years.

When the other side is seen as a threat and the game never ends, the team becomes more aggressive and insatiable. Our team tribalism is fueled by a sense of conviction that blinds us to our fellow citizens, to our own missteps, to the long-term consequences of our desire to win. In 2017 former speaker of the house John Boehner gave an honest and vulnerable interview with *Politico Magazine* and spoke about how prioritizing the team played out in his own career.[9] He spoke openly about both a huge budgetary reform and an immigration-reform package that had fallen apart because he prioritized his caucus over his country. At the end of the interview, one of Boehner's friends shared a poem as Boehner openly wept in the background.

A BUILDER OR A WRECKER

As I watched them tear a building down
A gang of men in a busy town
With a ho-heave-ho, and a lusty yell
They swung a beam and the side wall fell
I asked the foreman, "Are these men
    skilled,
And the men you'd hire if you wanted to
    build?"
He gave a laugh and said, "No, indeed,
Just common labor is all I need.
I can easily wreck in a day or two,
What builders have taken years to do."
And I thought to myself, as I went my
    way
Which of these roles have I tried to play
Am I a builder who works with care,
Measuring life by rule and square?
Am I shaping my work to a well-made
    plan
Patiently doing the best I can
Or am I a wrecker who walks to town
Content with the labor of tearing down?
"O Lord let my life and my labors be
That which will build for eternity!"[10]

We are "putting points on the board," but

62

are we building or wrecking? We might be building a winning team, but are we building anything that lasts? We are disconnecting from ourselves and our curiosity. We are giving up the opportunity to grow and adapt in our thoughts and beliefs. Despite staying tethered to our devices, we are unplugging from the world around us. By only looking through the lens of competition, we are losing the ability to see things as they really are. Most importantly, we are disconnecting from one another.

To (reluctantly) stay with sports metaphors, what's the long game? If we continue to believe that the other side is out to destroy America, wouldn't the only victory mean that 50 percent of the country packs up and goes elsewhere? That is not happening, and we would not be served if it did. We are here together. We aren't going anywhere. And we all belong. We have to find sources of connection despite our disagreement. In order to find that type of connection, we have to stop treating everything as a competition. We can stop focusing on racking up wins and reach out to each other in the face of our fear and anger and vulnerability. We can move forward together. We just have to take off our jerseys.

■ ■ ■ ■

Our jerseys make so many of our conversations predictable and, if we don't enjoy competitive sparring, exhausting. What's the point of talking to your neighbor about climate change if you know that one of you is going to say that the earth is on a downward and dangerous spiral and the other is going to say it's all a hoax? Why get into a conversation about health care at a dinner party if you know it will devolve into one side arguing for a nationalized system and the other arguing that market solutions are best?

Honestly, it's boring under the best of circumstances to communicate from our sides. But the two of us have found that taking off our jerseys can lead to much more interesting conversations, ones that strengthen our relationship and help us grow as people. As we continue to think and talk about welfare specifically, we've opened up new possibilities.

Often, we produce episodes that we refer to as "primers" in advance of our opinion shows. As we'll discuss in chapter 6, in primers we attempt to fully take off our jerseys and present purely factual information. Our goal is to establish a shared foundation of facts and context before we discuss our opinions on specific topics. We do extensive research to prepare these episodes and then try to distill that research into an easy-to-digest twenty-minute audio lesson.

When Sarah wanted to learn more about policymaking around poverty, she created a primer on welfare. She focused her research on the history of welfare in the United States and the welfare reform efforts of the 1990s. Through her research, she realized just how little she understood about how the system worked. For decades she had believed welfare provided a system of support for poverty-stricken families across the nation and that it deserved protection at all costs. Meanwhile, Beth saw welfare as a well-intended short-term measure that discouraged work, increased dependency, and had long outlived its usefulness. You've probably had these same conversations with friends and family, and we bet that the kinds of arguments the two of us repeated to each other were on loop in your houses too.

A history lesson was in order for both of us. That history lesson showed us that (1) most of us are a little bit right and a lot wrong on the facts surrounding welfare, and

(2) our partisan jerseys are preventing meaningful innovation to actually reduce poverty.

The many Americans who lament that welfare discourages work might be surprised to know that welfare began for the very purpose of preventing people from working. By "people," we mean "women," and more specifically "white women," and more specifically still, "white women who weren't divorced and hadn't had children outside of marriage." In other words, welfare began primarily as a way to support white widows who couldn't work because they were at home raising small children. This type of welfare, commonly known as "mothers' pensions," began at the state level. (How's that for turning our talking points on their heads? Welfare was designed by *states* to *prevent* women from working! There's something for everyone to love and hate.) Prior to the Great Depression, states provided these mothers with pensions, while local governments, churches, and charities tried to fill the remaining need.

But when the Great Depression hit and unemployment rose to levels that were unimaginable a decade earlier, state and local governments, even with the help of churches and charity organizations, simply couldn't keep up. On February 25, 1931, the *New York Times* reported that several hundred people smashed in the windows of a grocery and meat market in Minneapolis in order to take fruit, canned goods, and bacon. President Franklin D. Roosevelt determined that the federal government needed to step in. In his January 1935 address to Congress, he took a measured — dare we say *nuanced?* — stance on the federal government's responsibility toward its citizens as the nation worked toward recovery. He expressed a number of viewpoints we would regard today as utterly conflicting and confusing. In fact, his address embodied most of the modern salient talking points on welfare, but it did so from both "sides":

1. **He recognized systemic inequality.** "In spite of our efforts and in spite of our talk, we have not weeded out the overprivileged and we have not effectively lifted up the underprivileged."
2. **He also recognized the virtue in capitalism.** "No wise man has any intention of destroying what is known as the profit motive; because by the profit motive we mean the right by work to earn a decent livelihood for ourselves

and for our families."
3. **He promised to be a problem solver.** "To this end we are ready to begin to meet this problem — the intelligent care of population throughout our Nation, in accordance with an intelligent distribution of the means of livelihood for that population."
4. **But he recognized that the problem would not be solved overnight.** FDR described his program as one that would take "many future years to fulfill."
5. **He thought it critical to provide for people who could not provide for themselves.** "When humane considerations are concerned, Americans give them precedence."
6. **But he did not intend to create prolonged dependency on government relief.** "The lessons of history, confirmed by the evidence immediately before me, show conclusively that continued dependence upon relief induces a spiritual and moral disintegration fundamentally destructive to the national fibre. To dole out relief in this way is to administer a narcotic, a subtle destroyer of the human spirit."
7. **He also recognized a role for both**

states and the federal government. Individuals who could not care for themselves independently had previously been "cared for by local efforts — by states, by counties, by towns, by cities, by churches, and by private welfare agencies. It is my thought that in the future they must be cared for as they were before." Because the Depression had been a national crisis, FDR felt that the federal government needed to "give employment to all of these three and one half million employable people now on relief, pending their absorption in a rising tide of private employment."[11]

A fair reading of President Roosevelt's address makes it nearly impossible to wear a partisan jersey when it comes to welfare. He made the case that the citizens of the United States had just experienced an economic crisis tantamount to a national disaster, which required the US government to respond. He said that people needed to be provided for, but that they needed to be provided jobs, not unlimited cash relief that undermined their sense of self-determination. At the time during which the welfare state was created, there was no winning or losing solution. It was a crisis that required hard decisions, trade-offs, risks, and a willingness to adapt as circumstances changed.

Welfare began as a pragmatic solution to a problem (even if the problem was limited to white widowed mothers), but it has become a partisan football due at least in part to racism in the United States. Previously, the administration of mothers' pensions at the state level had allowed states to exclude black women from receiving assistance. According to Dylan Matthews writing for Vox .com,[12] black women were expected to continue working in domestic and agricultural jobs despite having children. However, with the rising civil rights movement and changing ideas about race, less discrimination was tolerated. This led to the expansion of the number of welfare recipients (because now welfare was available to more than just white mothers) and a ballooning of the welfare rolls. As more and more women worked outside the home, the idea that the government would pay some women, particularly black women, to stay home with their children was no longer seen as an obvious solution, but rather a source of resentment and frustration. The stereotypical "welfare queen" became a symbol of one more partisan battle royale.

Our culture had shifted, and paying people not to work — even mothers — was becoming untenable. For a moment, it seemed like both sides would take off their jerseys and find a solution. Democrats and Republicans agreed to work together on welfare reform during the Clinton administration. The resulting legislation, the Personal Responsibility and Work Opportunity Reconciliation Act of 1996, replaced most direct-cash benefits to the poor with block grants to states, imposed work requirements, and placed lifetime limits on the amount of assistance families could receive. In other words, welfare had been reformed to meet many of the arguments Republicans advanced.

And yet, despite congressional compromise and dramatic changes to our national welfare system, many of us still wear the jerseys of the 1980s while parroting the talking points of that time. Many of us, while either defending or deriding the philosophy behind them, still argue as if the federal government hands out cash benefits, which it no longer does. We argue as if there is *one* national welfare system, when the reality is that states have great freedom in how they distribute funds and have set up vastly different systems.

We are guilty of this ourselves. In our initial discussions about welfare, Sarah was a strident defender of what she still believed to be a national welfare system based around cash benefits. Despite her passionate beliefs about the system, however, she didn't have many interactions with it. Her history, education, and privileged background had insulated her from interacting with both the system and the people who use it. She knew very little about welfare reform and thought all negative opinions about the system were based on stereotypes and urban myths. Honest feedback from listeners about watching people in their families and neighborhoods exploit government benefits initially felt like an assault on a system she believed in. But Sarah listened with curiosity and learned to acknowledge that she didn't fully understand the system she was passionately supporting. Sarah realized that she had shut out concerns about punishing people who work, without learning the ins and outs of a system that even welfare advocates acknowledge encourages people to stay out of the workforce.

On the other hand, Beth, in typical Republican terms, had viewed welfare as a trap rather than a ladder. She believed that many people were being deprived of the dignity of work because they were stuck in a system that incentivized dependency. She viewed federal and state aid as a complicated web of bureaucracy that continued to add layers on top of expensive and ineffective layers, because politicians didn't want (and often weren't equipped) to make difficult decisions about which benefits should stay and which should go. Block grants to states made sense to her, because she had always viewed states as more effective problem solvers than the federal government. Beth was frustrated with Democrats who painted Republican objections to welfare as racist, classist, and heartless. She particularly objected to assertions that race was at play in welfare conversations; in her mind and heart, this discussion was about poverty for all people.

Learning about the history of welfare was an uncomfortably illuminating process for Beth. Seeing clearly the historical role race played in the attitudes she had adopted created a painful reckoning. Beth never intended to harbor racist attitudes about welfare, but many of the talking points that she had come to parrot had deep roots in Americans' unwillingness to provide the same public support for families of color as they had for white families. And digging into welfare reform helped Beth understand that most of the ideas she was advocating for had been tried, with disappointing and sometimes harmful results.

Our partisan jerseys had prevented a real understanding of the issues. They also had caused us to spend most of our energy not on analyzing and refining our own positions, but instead on demonizing our political opponents.

We had fallen into each of our party's misconceptions: Democrats seeing Republicans as wholly uncaring about the poor and Republicans believing Democrats entrap people in dependency in order to win elections. We'd approached the question of welfare as nothing other than "should people live off the government or not?" — an approach that ignores economic conditions and the balance of obligations between governments, the nonprofit sector, and the business community. Our team jerseys were so restricting that we didn't even see the complexity of various welfare programs, how and by whom they are administered, and what the objectives and outcomes have been. But, when we stopped to see past our jerseys, we had to ask ourselves, why on earth would we have "opponents" when talking about ensuring that our fellow

Americans are able to afford housing, food, and the basic necessities of life?

Substituting partisanship for problem-solving in formulating welfare policy has yielded ugly results. Today, we find ourselves with a social safety net that continues to explode the national deficit, that varies widely by state because of decisions on how to spend block grants, and that is less responsive to economic conditions than the programs of the 1930s. As Arthur Brooks, conservative commentator and former president of the American Enterprise Institute, has frequently noted, the "War on Poverty" (a phrase coined by President Lyndon Johnson during the 1960s and associated with the expansion of national welfare programs), combined with modern technology, has improved the conditions of being poor, but it has not made fewer people poor.[13]

Our partisan jerseys have been preventing a modern version of the conversation President Roosevelt advocated: a hard one about (1) what poverty looks like in America *right now,* (2) the future of work, (3) the fact that various welfare experiments can't be viewed fairly without analyzing the economic conditions at the times of those experiments, and (4) what our values as Americans are. We have had major blinders on. We have viewed data, when we have it at all, through the lens of confirmation bias. We have limited our creativity in thinking about what we can actually do about poverty, because we've been stuck in a conversation solely about whether to protect or dismantle federal welfare programs.

We've also mostly ignored the fact that the world has changed dramatically since the late 1990s. Because we've been wearing partisan jerseys, we've stayed on the same field; meanwhile, the *actual* world as experienced by people living on about two dollars in cash each day has been transformed. Taking off our jerseys has helped both of us see the *real* field so that we can ask better questions.

For example, technology has dramatically reduced the traditional job opportunities available for low-skilled workers. In an article for *Fortune* magazine, Barb Darrow noted that "an estimated 5 million U.S. factory jobs have evaporated since 2000 and most of those (88%) were lost to increased productivity due to automation, according to a study by Ball State University."[14] And it's not just (or even primarily) that technology has rendered jobs obsolete; it's that available jobs require a higher degree of skill. In the first quarter of 2017, 45 percent of small businesses reported that they couldn't find qualified applicants to work in their companies.

Chief executive officers report shortages of workers for middle-class-wage jobs such as nurses, construction workers, truck drivers, oilfield workers, automotive technicians, industrial technicians, heavy equipment operators, computer network support specialists, web developers and insurance specialists. If these types of jobs go unfilled, businesses will expand more slowly and U.S. growth will be impeded.[15]

What would it mean for welfare to look more like supporting people through technical and apprenticeship training so that they are qualified to fill these jobs? Taking off her jersey has helped Beth see that this was part of the intention of the Clinton administration. When he talked about ending welfare "as we know it today," Clinton envisioned a country with universal health care, childcare subsidies, and a host of other support systems. Republicans in Congress derailed those aspects of the Clinton agenda, so the welfare reform that took place was like offering up one piece of a fairly complicated puzzle.

Removing her partisan jersey has also helped Beth see work requirements through a more nuanced lens. In 2017 the Trump administration advocated for states to seek waivers from the Centers for Medicare and Medicaid Services to add work requirements for Medicaid recipients, a practice that is being advocated for in our home state of Kentucky. This feels like a retread of Clintonian welfare-reform efforts. It sounds great to talk about work requirements, but consider the types of jobs that are available, what those jobs pay, and what successfully performing those jobs requires. When President Roosevelt talked about the necessity of work, he meant that the government would create jobs that paid well enough to give people new leases on life. When we talk about job requirements today, we mean, "go find something that exists in the private sector and that you're qualified to do today, even if it doesn't pay wages that enable you to deal with transportation, childcare, and all the other aspects of your life that must be well managed in order for you to do and keep your job."

It's almost trite to talk about education as the answer to poverty, but looking at both poverty data and our educational institutions without a jersey helps us see that we haven't really tried this solution. As a country, we have a near-obsession with four-year college degrees — degrees that are taking longer than four years to secure at much higher costs, driving students into levels of debt that make a standard of living that is higher than their parents' seem like a fantasy. American debates about primary education are always heated, but they always seem to be versions of the same questions. We're constantly asking how to produce more "career-ready" students and depending on our schools to be the entirety of that answer, without asking what reforms are needed in parenting, in business, in spirituality, in our approaches to mental health. As Audrey Watters wrote in "The Invented History of 'The Factory Model of Education' ":

We tend to not see automation today as *mechanization* as much as *algorithmization* — the promise and potential in artificial intelligence and virtualization, as if this magically makes these new systems of standardization and control lighter and liberatory.

And so too we've invented a history of "the factory model of education" in order to justify an "upgrade" — to new software and hardware that will do much of the same thing schools have done for generations now, just (supposedly) more efficiently, with control moved out of the hands of labor (teachers) and into the hands of a new class of engineers, out of the realm of the government and into the realm of the market.[16]

Taking off our jerseys about education (where we tend to be either pro– or anti–teachers' unions and pro– or anti–Common Core — usually from places of gross misinformation, which we'll return to in chapter 3) enables us to see the larger and shifting field at play in a way that's necessarily entangled with poverty. First and foremost, we need to start thinking about education as a lifelong endeavor. The people who have been willing to make this shift are offering some interesting potential roadmaps. For example, Republican governor Bill Haslam led Tennessee's Drive to 55. This initiative was a bold commitment to "get 55 percent of Tennesseans equipped with a college degree or certificate by the year 2025"[17] and contained specific initiatives for adults who need to finish degrees or learn new skills. What is Drive to 55 other than an innovation in our modern conception of welfare? It might not be perfect or complete, and certainly we'll learn more about its impact in the coming years. But it is a step in asking new questions about how we can actually reduce poverty in the United States.

Cultural issues have also changed the field in the welfare debate. Beginning with mothers' pensions, much of the old welfare debate has centered on marriage. Conservative critiques of welfare have often decried welfare's disincentives to marry. Although studies still confirm the value of married parents to outcomes for children,[18] it's impossible to ignore the fact that attitudes about marriage have changed dramatically over the past few decades. Our understanding of the roles of mothers and fathers is changing. Our understanding of who might have children and how they might have children is changing. And, very significantly, people are living longer (which has upended Social Security, and it's impossible to have a thoughtful discussion about poverty in America without discussing the entirety of the social safety net). Consequently, caregiving is a growing need, and yet it is a multi-generational endeavor that is completely at odds with the workaholic culture pervasive in corporate America. All these factors come into play when we think about poverty.

Taking off our jerseys allows us to ask questions and grapple with the web of factors that causes poverty to persist in one of the earth's wealthiest nations. It has also helped us clarify our own values so that we can precisely articulate our concerns and ideas. We have both come to see the value of cash assistance. Sarah has started thinking about the condescension of in-kind benefits — why do we think we know what people need better than they do? A listener sent us a message about the sometimes-nonsensical requirements of using welfare benefits for educational programs that drove home the necessity of easing federal control over personal choices.

Also, Beth has become clear on the fact that she isn't worried about abuse of the system. When a listener wrote a heartfelt message about people close to her who took advantage of welfare without trying to improve their circumstances, Beth responded:

I had to think about this message for a few days to get clear on my own response. I don't think that anything you say here is wrong or overstated or unusual. Many people find themselves needing assistance and support because of bad decisions repeated over a lifetime. Many people program shop. Many people abuse the system. Many people misdirect resources. Many people don't try to improve their circumstances.

Here's my perspective: I choose not to think about this.

The reality is that these same bad decisions, abuses of the system, etc., can happen regardless of the structure of the system. And I have made a really deliberate choice in my life to prioritize grace over fairness. That's not the right decision for everyone, and I'm not saying that my personal preferences always make sound policy. But this is where I am.

I choose grace. So even though many people create their own circumstances (some over and over and over again), I want them to have a place to live and food to eat and the opportunity to live with more ease even if they will likely blow that opportunity. I choose not to think about cigarettes or televisions or iPhones or how hard someone works compared to how hard I work. That search for justice makes me miserable and gets me nowhere. I can't control anyone's choices, motivation, or path, and I certainly don't think government can. That's why I'm leaning more toward universal basic income. Let's dismantle the layers of administrators designed to essentially control people and just provide them with charity and the opportunity to later repay that charity by contributing to the system.

Again, this is in no way a criticism of your position, which is valid and one I understand. This is just where I am.[19]

With these understandings and the questions that we were able to ask once we took off our jerseys, we both have started giving serious consideration to the idea of a universal basic income, as Beth mentioned to that listener. Michelle Chen described the idea of universal basic income (UBI) as "radically simple":

The UBI model is . . . a basic payment designed to cover basic expenses. After giving to each according to need, people are freer to give according to ability. UBIvangelists argue that automatically providing for basic nutritional and shelter needs liberates people to ascend the hierarchy of needs and focus on more valuable activities, like developing social relationships and civic and cultural engagement. Others hope a UBI would foster a more harmonious, cooperative post-work society simply by countering scarcity and selfishness.[20]

It might not be (and probably isn't) the perfect solution. We maintain some skepticism and concern about this idea being advanced in light of technology as the center of our economy. There is more to life and to the American economy than Silicon Valley, and we worry a little that tech giants are increasingly pervasive forces in our civic dialogue. Any attempts to implement a universal basic income would need serious consideration, debate, and study, and should be viewed through a lens that is broader than the belief that the American economy will be driven forever by technology. We don't have all the details mapped out, but we see it as a possible way to ensure that our fellow Americans maintain a certain standard of living along with liberty and dignity, to help adjust to an ever-changing economy, to eliminate some well-intended bureaucracy and some old fights over various conceptions of morality, and, hopefully, alongside other programs, to help people in need improve their circumstances.

Most significantly, because universal basic income is such a new concept, there aren't "team" positions on it yet. We can't put on our jerseys because no one knows how the parties will choose to handle this issue. That freedom from the entrenched ideas and policy positions that usually come with the jerseys has enabled us to home in on our shared values rather than our differences. We agree, as it turns out, on many points:

- The goal of welfare should be to help people improve their circumstances in the long-term and survive the short-term.
- There is a baseline-level standard of living that we want all Americans to have.
- Both federal and state governments have roles to play in this discussion (which is a meaningful level of agreement even though we maintain differences on scope and emphasis for each).
- Our current system is not working in part because it has limited cash assistance.
- Cash assistance is sometimes abused, but we will accept some abuse in order to make the effort of living out our values.
- People receiving benefits should not sacrifice the agency of making their

own decisions in exchange for those benefits.

We could never have reached these agreements or approached any potential solutions while wearing our partisan jerseys. Team jerseys limit us, rather than equip us to harness the power of our ideological diversity for the purpose of developing solutions to complicated and evolving problems. The jerseys keep us on the same field, playing the same games, trying to win the same arguments. They ensure that we get stuck in the past, putting points on the board as the game itself becomes irrelevant. When we stop trying to win, we are able to think, experiment, learn, and innovate.

Taking off our partisan jerseys is essential to good policymaking, but policy is just the beginning. Removing our jerseys can help us understand not only what laws we want passed but also what kind of people we are and what kind of country we want to live in. It is essential to living out our values, which, at the end of the day, is what we're all trying to do as we have these difficult conversations and decide how to govern our lives. The central tenet of almost every tradition of faith or virtue is that we are all one and should treat each other lovingly. We appreciate how Richard Rohr explained the trinity as embodying this concept for us as Christians:

> Trinity represents the overcoming of the foundational philosophical problem called "the One and the Many." How things are both utterly connected and yet distinct is invariably the question of the serious seeker. In the paradigm of Trinity, we have three autonomous "Persons," as we call them, who are nevertheless in perfect communion. It is a new definition of unity and a protection of diversity too, which offers us a template for everything else. We must hold the tension between distinct individuals and absolute communion. That's the only way we'll survive in this world, it seems to me. Each person in the Trinity is totally autonomous and yet totally given and surrendered to the others. With the endless diversity in creation, it is clear that God is *not* obsessed with uniformity. God does not desire uniformity, but unity. Unity is diversity embraced by an infinitely generous love.[21]

Partisan jerseys are inherently disconnecting, running afoul of historic and enduring teachings of faith. By behaving as though our identities as Republicans or Democrats define us, we are defining ourselves oppositionally: "I am because I am against my neighbors who think differently." That is not who we were created to be.

This is not to say that people of virtue or faith should not identify with political parties. There is nothing inherently wrong with group affiliation. But there *is* something tremendously wrong with prioritizing our differences over our sameness and abdicating our personal responsibility to independently consider and act on issues in favor of following the group's checklist. We talked with Michael Wear, author of *Reclaiming Hope* and former Obama administration official, about this in January 2018 and came to express our responsibility as people of faith this way: participating in the political process is a spiritual imperative, but we should participate as an *expression* of our faith, not as a fulfillment of our faith. In other words, faith or values should inform rather than define our votes, opinions, and ways of talking with our neighbors about the future of the country. When we're participating, as Michael says, with our feet grounded in our values, there is no room for bitter partisanship.[22]

Challenging ourselves to take off our jerseys doesn't have to mean we are wrong or that our hearts have been in the wrong place. It can illuminate all that we're missing because of our affiliation. We have been thinking about the story told in Matthew (26:6–13), Mark (14:3–9), Luke (7:36–50), and John (12:1–8) of the woman who poured expensive oil from an alabaster flask onto Jesus' feet. The Gospel writers noted that the disciples rebuked her for using the ointment rather than selling it and giving the proceeds to the poor. That is some well-intended and self-righteous jersey wearing! The disciples loved their own dedication to the poor in the same ways that many of us on both sides of the aisle do — Democrats who protect and defend federal welfare programs and Republicans who expound on the dignity of work.

But Jesus told the disciples they had missed the big picture, explaining that the woman had prepared his body for burial. In Mark's telling, Jesus said, "She has done what she could."[23] This description should be our aspiration for civic participation — not that we have been forceful defenders of a party line, no matter how compelling that party line, but that we have done what we could, that we have considered what we have to offer and offered it humbly and without expectation. When we're wearing our jerseys, we're not doing what we can; we're just mimicking what others tell us about what must be.

1. Consider aspects of your life in which you've been unable to see the big picture because of group affiliation. Begin outside of politics. Have you been a parent in the stands at a sports event who forgot about sportsmanship in "cheering on" your children? Have you chosen a side in a conflict at work, at school, or in church and lost the ability to treat those on the other side with kindness and respect?
2. As you move into your political life, think about the candidates you have supported. Do those candidates represent the values most important to you, or do they merely wear your preferred jersey?
3. When you think about members of the other party, do you view them as neighbors? When you think about America's involvement in the world, are you looking at citizens of other countries as your neighbors?

CHAPTER THREE:
FIND YOUR WHY

Once we've taken off our jerseys and decided that the team isn't our priority, what's next? What happens when we attempt to actually leave the playing field in pursuit of something larger? If the primary desire is no longer to win, what is there? If we aren't a member of the team, who are we? If we take off the jersey, what will we find underneath?

The answer to all these questions comes down to one fundamental question: Why? Why do I care? Why is an issue important to me? Why do I support this policy? What outcome am I actually looking for? Why do I support this candidate? Why have I held on tightly to this position?

Leaving these questions unasked has left a void. It has allowed us to let politicians, issues, and controversies stand in for our values, resulting in disconnection from our fellow citizens and from ourselves. Political parties have become the cause rather than the effect of values for many of us. This is, to think of it biblically, like building our houses on sand. Our values are the rocks that should serve as our foundation — helping us weather all the controversy, change, and challenges of current events. From those rocks, we can construct policy positions, find our ways into parties that most closely align with those policy positions, and test our parties and candidates against those values.

Too many of us are skipping those steps and substituting the parties' values for our own in the name of winning numbers games to "take control of the House" or "start a blue wave." Beth loves the television show *Survivor* but worries that we're starting to think of voting in the same bare terms that *Survivor* contestants use to "make sure our alliance has the numbers." Our driving force shouldn't be ensuring that a particular party controls a particular wing of government. Our driving force should be the values that are most important to us in living in community with other people.

When we take off our jerseys, we can start to see parties as they are: collections of policy positions animated by political personalities. We start to see how we as citizens and a country use them as cheap imitations of core values, how we use them as a shortcut for our own soul-searching and analysis. This is evident particularly with presidential candidates who become the embodiment of their political parties and their party members' values. The GOP isn't the party of small government. It's the party of Reagan. And Democrats' idolization of Obama stretched so far as to become the entire identity of certain groups inside the party, like the "Obama Bros."

We understand feeling the pull of certain political personalities, and there's nothing inherently wrong with that. Sarah dedicated a year of her life to working for Hillary Clinton in 2007 and makes no apologies for her devotion. Beth snapped a photograph of Sarah weeping in excitement as Clinton accepted the Democratic nomination for president in 2016 in Philadelphia. The photo beautifully reflects how profoundly impacted and deeply inspired we can feel when we gravitate to certain political personalities. But it's one thing to be a fan of politicians; it is another to become a follower. Followers substitute political figures' judgment for their own, excuse inexcusable behavior, and often accept unacceptable versions of events simply to toe the line with their preferred representatives. Politicians shouldn't determine our positions and values. Our values should determine the policies and politicians we support. When we don't understand our "why" — the values behind our positions — we are too easily tempted to follow our confirmation bias down an amoral or immoral black hole of support for politicians who simply don't deserve it.

Another easy shortcut we use for our values is issues — particularly controversial social issues. Even when we fundamentally misunderstand issues, we hold fast to them as though they are critical expressions of our morality. *Education Next (EdNext)*, an education policy journal, conducts an annual poll. Their findings regarding Common Core State Standards are an excellent manifestation of our abandoning the why and using policy positions as substitutes for our values. In 2012 *EdNext* asked about Common Core State Standards, which are intended to establish consistent educational objectives in all US states. That year, 90 percent of those polled supported the standards.[1] By 2016 only half of respondents supported Common Core — a dramatic decline. However, when *EdNext* asked about "the use of the same standards across states" without using the actual term "Common Core," two-thirds of respondents said they approved. In both political parties, the description of Common Core polled higher than the term "Common Core," and the difference was even more dramatic among Republicans.[2] *EdNext*'s polling shows that we aren't having conversations that lead to a deep understanding of *why* we oppose Common Core. We fundamentally don't understand what Common Core is.

Of course, these types of policy conversations are practically absent from the national conversation, because there's no need to talk about specific policy if your why is advancing your political party at the other party's expense. The Tyndall Report tracks each of the major networks' nightly news broadcasts and tallies the total amount of time spent on substantive policy discussions during elections. In 2008, news programs dedicated 220 minutes to policy. In 2012, the amount of time had dropped to 114 minutes. By October 2016, a mere 32 minutes were dedicated to in-depth discussion of policy — both foreign and domestic.[3] In December 2016, the Shorenstein Center on Media, Politics, and Public Policy noted that 10 percent of total press coverage during the election focused on policy.[4]

Candidates are tracking this trend. Despite Hillary Clinton being a self-identified policy wonk, only 25 percent of Clinton's more than $1 billion of ads discussed policy — compared to the traditional 40 percent from past presidential candidates.[5]

We have allowed real dialogue about the role of government and substantive discussions about solutions to our most pressing problems to become extinct. We should not be okay with that. How can we move forward in a fruitful way without taking the time to think and converse on a deeper level? We have to figure out why we care about abortion or why Obamacare ignites our rage. We have to examine our blind support for the social safety net and our mistrust of government. We have to ask ourselves hard questions about the role of our military and when foreign aid is appropriate. We have to delve deep into the issues so that we can find the values lurking below the surface, our whys.

Your why is often closely connected to your identity, loved ones, life experiences, and traditions. We are not asking you to change those things, to give up your fundamental values. On the contrary, we're asking you to embrace those values more wholeheartedly and to hold your parties and representatives to higher standards. We are asking you (1) to be clear about what your fundamental values are, and (2) to be clear about why you have arranged your politics around those values as you have. Why does a party that speaks to your values on one particular issue of importance inform all your other policy positions? Why does that issue occupy such a place of importance to you?

We have to let go of the idea that there is too much at stake or that one issue is too important to honestly and realistically question our positions on other issues. Abandoning our whys and allowing politicians or single-policy goals to stand in for our values keeps the stakes too high. It means we can never focus on a bigger perspective where values such as liberty and equality are dynamically playing out across our communities and country — instead we must be willing to sacrifice *everything* for this election or that legislative fight that has come to represent all we hold dear.

But, in theory, we live in a democracy for reasons that are more fundamental and enduring than taking "control" of the Supreme Court or changing certain laws. It's important to ask ourselves what we value about America. When we frame up our participation in a democracy, what core beliefs matter to us? It might sound basic to start naming values like liberty, equality, and justice. However, without these fundamentals, our government has become rudderless. Our Congress acts like a business or nonprofit with no mission statement; short-term revenue in the form of reelection next November becomes the goal, and no one ever asks, "Reelection in service of what?" Defining our values allows us to move past a transactional view of politics, which has us too focused on maintaining our ground, and instead gives us plenty of opportunities to look at issues with fresh eyes, trained on the things we hold most dear rather than clouded by old allegiances.

Getting to these fundamental whys can involve difficult introspection. When we name our values clearly and start to test issues and candidates against those values, sometimes ideas and people we have vigorously supported will fail those tests. Sometimes we find ourselves feeling critical of people we're accustomed to defending. Sometimes it makes us realize that we don't have enough information to test a policy or person against our values. And sometimes it requires us to think differently about the experiences in our lives that form the basis of our values. That can be uncomfortable, and it can leave us feeling vulnerable and afraid of being exploited.

But finding our why is essential. Using "winning" as our why *isn't working* for our country, our parties, our politicians, or ourselves.

Beth attended an event not long ago with people she loves very much. She sat on the floor playing with her younger daughter, who preferred reading books to playing with the other kids. Adults in the room, munching on carrot sticks and sausage balls, started talking about doctor's appointments, various maladies, and prescription drugs. Eventually health insurance came up, and the uncomfortable dance of talking without "getting political" commenced.

You've probably had this experience. It's hard to talk about health care because very few of us can get to a why at the core of a national debate. If we have a serious health issue or love someone with a serious health issue, it's hard to see past mounting bills, long waiting-room visits, and the fears that accompany illness. If we are relatively healthy, perhaps we think mostly about our premiums and our taxes. But these are concerns, not values from which good policy can spring.

Since the Clinton administration, we've been debating health care in extreme terms without making material progress on the cost of care, the outcomes of care, and a sustainable system for access to care. We keep arguing. Meanwhile premiums continue to rise. Health insurers continue to consolidate. Too many of our citizens do not have consistent and affordable access to high-quality health care. Nearly everyone laments the experience of being a patient in America. And yet we struggle to come to the table and have thoughtful, civil discussions on what to do about the problem.

During 1993 and 1994, the Health Insurance Association of America spent well over eight figures on the "Harry and Louise ads," depicting a futuristic couple grappling with the fallout from a government health-care takeover.[6] One such ad said ominously, "If we let the government choose, we lose."[7] Those ads appear quaint compared to the vitriol that followed when President Obama introduced the Affordable Care Act (ACA). "Obamacare," as Republicans derisively branded it, drew hundreds of Tea Party activists to town hall meetings. At one such event, the father of a man with cerebral palsy accused Democratic representative

John Dingell of "order[ing] a death sentence" for his son.[8] On August 7, 2009, former Republican vice-presidential nominee Sarah Palin shared a Facebook post containing what would become a central talking point in the health-care debate:

As more Americans delve into the disturbing details of the nationalized health care plan that the current administration is rushing through Congress, our collective jaw is dropping, and we're saying not just no, but hell no!

The Democrats promise that a government health care system will reduce the cost of health care, but as the economist Thomas Sowell has pointed out, government health care will not reduce the cost; it will simply refuse to pay the cost. And who will suffer the most when they ration care? The sick, the elderly, and the disabled, of course. The America I know and love is not one in which my parents or my baby with Down Syndrome will have to stand in front of Obama's "death panel" so his bureaucrats can decide, based on a subjective judgment of their "level of productivity in society," whether they are worthy of health care. Such a system is downright evil.[9]

Despite Palin's statement becoming Politi-Fact's Lie of the Year,[10] the "death panels" talking point stuck. Americans across the country railed against what they believed was a government that would literally choose who received critical treatments and who didn't. The length and complexity of the Affordable Care Act didn't help a bitterly partisan divide over the bill (neither did Nancy Pelosi's often-quoted-out-of-context statement that Congress needed to pass the bill so that the Americans could see what's in it outside the "fog of controversy").

It seemed that the Obamacare protests and outrage had to be the pinnacle of polarized discourse. Yet a few years later, when congressional Republicans and the Trump administration set out to repeal the Affordable Care Act, Americans defended the ACA with a similar existential fury. In July 2017 a group of health activists bused protestors to the homes of senators Rob Portman and John Boozman. Disability advocates were arrested for staging a "die-in" in the Capitol building, and images of police officers handcuffing and removing individuals with physical disabilities flooded the media.

We are what we practice, and in America,

we have practiced bitter partisan debates carried out in the most extreme terms possible — all framed in the context of a single question: Should health insurance be administered primarily by the federal government or not?

Coming from opposite ends of the ideological spectrum, we knew we had very different answers to that question. Sarah brought absolute conviction in the Affordable Care Act and was open to it as a first step toward a single-payer system, in which taxes finance a single public system that provides essential health care to all residents. Sarah also felt that the profit motives of insurance and pharmaceutical companies were skewing the entire health-care system in ways that disadvantaged everyone. In her mind, a purely market-based solution to situations in which a vast majority of Americans don't "shop" around (or, as she says, no one searches for the cheapest ambulance before they call 911) had created a system rife for exploitation. Beth, on the other hand, had real problems with the ACA, viewing it as federal overreach — a massive expansion of bureaucracy that had been ill conceived and poorly executed. But she felt guarded coming into the discussion, having too frequently experienced Democrats discussing any objection to the ACA as greedy, shameful, and even wishing for poor people to die.

We wondered how we might find any common ground and carry out a productive conversation. Starting with why was key. We decided to dive into the emotional and spiritual issues at the core of questions about health care, rather than starting and getting stuck on health insurance. It was difficult to unpack our values around health care (and it's an ongoing discussion to which we often return), but it has taught us two very important things: (1) we have more agreement than disagreement, and (2) substantially improving health care in America requires a much broader discussion than whether the federal government has a role to play in administering health insurance.

Returning to Sarah Palin's "death panels" for a moment offers a road map — not to good policy, but to good conversation. Why is the conversation on health care so emotionally charged? This debate represents different values for different groups. Almost all of us approach this debate with our values wrapped in an enormous amount of fear about our bodies, our families, and our economic security (and, deep down, probably death). Given that fear is not a prescription for problem-solving, we decided to approach the values underlying health care first.

The principal value that Sarah was bringing to health-care discussions was fairness. She saw the massive profits on one end of the system and the massive costs borne on the other and couldn't help but feel frustration and anger. She felt genuine empathy for all Americans and didn't want any family to have to choose between a doctor's visit and groceries. She didn't want any family to be bankrupted by an illness, and she didn't want any parent to worry that the treatment a child needed was unaffordable. Sarah's compassion led her to prioritize the issue of affordable care — or the absence of it — and she viewed it as a problem requiring the strength and resources of the federal government, which, for all its flaws, is not driven by profit.

The principal value that Beth was bringing to health-care discussions was federalism. She worried about how a nationalized health-care system could respond to specific needs state by state and how moving in that direction might impact other rights. In our home state of Kentucky, Beth had observed the difficulty state legislators had in dealing with requirements and resources for hospitals in rural versus urban and suburban areas. She feared that the raging debates over funding for abortion and contraception — as well as debates on other charged issues impacting women's health and transgender health care — would escalate further if taxpayer funding underwrote everyone's health care. She also saw the federal government as incapable of effectively administering health plans. How could a federal insurance program quickly respond to changes in the delivery of care? How could patient data be protected in such a system?

When we stepped back from the "how" (federal intervention or the private system of insurance), we found that our whys were identical. Both of us wanted high-quality health care at affordable prices for all Americans. Like Sarah, Beth didn't want anyone to suffer from inadequate care, and she didn't want families to have to make excruciating decisions because of injury or illness. As we discussed this topic, the parable of the good Samaritan kept coming up for Beth. How could she reconcile her beliefs about what a federal system can and can't accomplish with her deeply held conviction that we are all here to be neighbors to one another — that we are all to stop on the path without excuses, carry the sick to places of healing, and pay for that care with quiet, generous hearts?

Knowing that we wanted affordable care for everyone, we decided next to talk about what that care actually looked like — a question we both felt was ignored in most health-care policy enacted in the past several decades. We found that we wanted a system dictated by patient values rather than by "what my insurance will cover." We found that the imbalance of power between the medical community and the patient bothered us both tremendously. We found that we weren't just bothered by the cost of care, but also by the quality of care in the American health-care system. We also both realized our perspectives were significantly informed by our experiences with maternity care and end-of-life decisions.

Throughout our pregnancies, we'd had the resources to do enormous amounts of research. Beth always tells people that she studied harder for labor than she did for two bar exams, and between us, we have a library on pregnancy, birth, and breastfeeding. We realized that what insurance covers for pregnancy and birth didn't always align with our values. We wanted to be treated like pregnant women going through a natural, healthy human condition instead of patients presenting with an illness. Sarah wanted to have her children at home (so did Beth, but that's a story for another day). We both wanted to have our children with as few interventions as possible. When Sarah dealt with a miscarriage, she wanted to discuss as many options as possible and deal with that loss as a loss, rather than as a condition requiring treatment. When Beth's baby was breech in month nine, she wanted to talk about options to move the baby rather than scheduling a C-section.

We both ultimately had births without pain medication and with healthy children — but it required us to employ our educational and financial resources. We were able to pay out of pocket for chiropractic care, massage therapy, doulas, and midwives. We were able to advocate for ourselves using our training as lawyers when we disagreed with doctors' recommendations. This was a springboard of serious agreement for us. We found common ground around the principle that a woman shouldn't need a law degree, research abilities, and disposable income to have a positive pregnancy and birth experience. We also had an important realization. Because we approached our pregnancies and births as a part of life instead of as pathology, they cost our insurers substantially less. What impact might it make if our health-care system broadly empowered women to understand their options and make decisions about maternity care?

Instead care is seen as something to consume, not something to engage in. In America more care is always better care. This phenomenon seems to create both a culture of scarcity and a culture that is overprescribed and overtreated. We constantly worry about whether we'll be able to pay for the care we need, while at the same time defining "need" very broadly. We've determined that if we have any symptoms, they must be treated with the maximum care available. In his article "Overkill," Atul Gawande wrote:

In 2010, the Institute of Medicine issued a report stating that waste accounted for thirty percent of health-care spending, or some seven hundred and fifty billion dollars a year, which was more than our nation's entire budget for K-12 education. The report found that higher prices, administrative expenses, and fraud accounted for almost half of this waste. Bigger than any of those, however, was the amount spent on unnecessary health-care services. Now a far more detailed study confirmed that such waste was pervasive.[11]

Gawande explained the prevalence of overtesting and the two disturbing outcomes it creates: (1) heightened levels of cancer in the population because we're conducting so many forms of radiation imaging, and (2) overdiagnosis — that is, correctly diagnosing issues in the body that would never have manifested in significant ways absent their discovery and unnecessarily treating those issues.

We can relate to Gawande's findings. Beth had to fight with a hospital to release her daughter Jane three days after she was born. The hospital pediatrician wanted to keep Jane multiple nights following her birth because her bilirubin levels were slightly elevated. When Beth asked for specifics, she learned that the pediatrician was using bilirubin levels for a premature baby as his baseline. Jane had been born fourteen days after her estimated due date. When Beth insisted on signing an "against medical advice" form to be released, the nursing staff tried to persuade her otherwise. It wasn't until she shared that she was a lawyer and fully understood the ramifications that they made arrangements for both Beth and Jane to go home. Beth immediately took Jane to the physician who would be Jane's long-term pediatrician. That physician was astonished and annoyed that Jane and Beth had been hospitalized for so long for no real reason. Beth (under her high-deductible plan) and her health insurance company incurred several thousand dollars in costs for unnecessary treatment. She also lost skin-to-skin time with Jane because the physician insisted that Jane be placed under lights and wear goggles. And the entire family experienced the discomfort, intrusion, and inconvenience of an extra hospital stay. We wish this experience wasn't so disturbingly common.

This phenomenon of overdiagnosis and overtreatment helps explain the confounding statistic that the United States spends more on health care than any other country (whether you measure that spending per capita or as a percentage of overall wealth). On average other countries spend about half as much as the United States spends, and that gap has been steadily widening every year since 1980.[12] Despite this spending, our outcomes are not better than countries under other health-care systems. We have higher rates of hospitalization for preventable diseases than comparable countries; higher rates of medical, medication, or lab errors or delays than comparable countries; and slower rates of access to doctors or nurses than comparable countries.[13]

Taking all the information available to us, we agreed that Americans are probably receiving too much care. We recognize that is a hard message, especially for anyone who has dealt with or is currently enduring a significant medical issue. We aren't trying to demonize doctors or patients. We appreciate medical professionals and are thankful for the research and tools they bring to the table when those tools are needed. We don't want anyone to go without the care they need. But we do think it's important for patients and the medical community to discuss values around health care.

In addition to thinking that Americans are probably receiving too much health care, we found agreement on other issues that increase costs. We think it would be helpful under any health insurance system for prices to be presented to patients in writing in advance of treatments in non-emergency situations. While you can't shop for an ambulance, there are plenty of circumstances while seeking health care where price shopping would be appropriate. Congress has required restaurants to put calorie counts on menus, yet during a doctor's visit a patient might be escorted to an X-ray room after complaining of minor pain with no opportunity to consider the costs. More transparency in pricing is not a new idea, and it's one we think should be seriously considered in any health-care reform efforts.

We also believe that we're defining health care too narrowly in large part due to insurance companies. The push for greater wellness under the Affordable Care Act and many company policies has largely been about preventative medicine (i.e., receiving an annual physical, mammogram, etc.). These are important first steps. What would it be like, though, if our culture embraced greater prevention in the form of regular therapy, massage, acupuncture, and other forms of treatment that reduce stress? After all, since the 1980s, we've been talking about stress as an American epidemic, responsible for back pain, persistent headaches, circulatory problems, and increased violence.[14] Rethinking the ways that we support ourselves and one another is a critical step toward reducing disease and conditions that consume enormous health-care resources today.

Having defined some of our values and concerns around health care, we then were able to have a more productive conversation about health insurance and the government's role in the health insurance system. In this conversation, we agreed not to talk about the Affordable Care Act as an all-or-nothing proposition. We frequently analogize the ACA to the woods. The woods are neither good nor bad; there are beautiful trees, dangerous animals, singing birds, and thick areas of brush that are difficult to navigate. That's how the ACA is. The legislation spanned roughly 2,300 pages when it was passed, not counting more than 20,000 pages of regulations later promulgated to effectuate it. There is too much going on to say that it's all good or all bad.

We disagreed about the individual mandate but found lots of space for agreement. Because we wanted greater transparency in pricing, more flexibility in what we spend health care dollars on, and more accessible health care for everyone, we agreed that the ACA's individual marketplace concept is a good step toward unhooking health insurance from employment. We also agreed that the ACA's emphasis on employer-sponsored health plans is the wrong direction in health-care law, that it undermines the individual marketplaces, and that overall it works against the goals of reducing costs and increasing access.

We saw employer-sponsored health plans as relics of the past that bear no relevance to the modern economy, that limit choice and transparency, and that are a lose-lose proposition for both employers and employees. Employers continue to deal with rising costs of premiums. Employees often complain about the options and costs of employer-sponsored plans or feel trapped in positions because of their plans. Meanwhile, insurers are not serving or negotiating directly with health-care consumers. Their customers are employers. As a number of conservative commentators, and particularly Avik Roy, have pointed out, this limits competitive pressure on insurers in terms of both pricing and service:

More portability wouldn't only liberate workers, it would also rearrange incentives for insurers. If an insurer thought it might keep a 25-year-old patient for another 40 years, it would want to work with the patient to be healthier, with free checkups, a deeper discount on cholesterol medicine, fitness programs etc.[15]

Our sticking point remained the role of the federal government. Beth understood the individual mandate but thought it was government overreach. Sarah thought a single-payer system would solve the problem of employer-based health care, but we both worried about what would happen in a single-payer system in terms of administration, women's health care, and the quality of care. Breaking down our areas of agreement and disagreement did not make health-care policy less complex. It did make discussing health-care policy productive and manageable. The two of us aren't going to solve this issue, but we think we did solve the problem of shaming and blaming other people about health care to a point that closes off fertile ground for consensus policy proposals.

Fortunately, we aren't required to figure out a comprehensive legislative or cultural fix for our health-care system. We are simply here to start that conversation afresh. Beth has conceded that "keeping government out of health care" is not a value for her. It's fine to bring the framework of federalism to these discussions, but it cannot be the only consideration. Sarah has conceded that a single-payer system would not solve every problem, and while it might remain her preferred course of action, she sees possibilities for improving the system overall that stop short of single-payer. And we've both learned more about our own values and each other's values when it comes to health care. Without examining *why* we want health care to be accessible and affordable, we can't get to *how* in an accurate and complete way. Once we understand our why, then we can reach the how.

Finding our whys also helped illuminate for us the importance of individuals and institutions closely examining a number of positions relevant to health care. The "death panels" controversy has helped us understand that many Americans are concerned about losing the ability to make health-care decisions — which is a fair concern, but it's not accurate and complete unless we talk about the power of insurance companies. It's also not an accurate and complete concern without examining other positions we stake out that impact health care — particularly issues of life, death, and identity.

Anytime we talk about our values, we are drawn back to our faith and to institutions of faith. We're concerned that the voice of the church in America has been devoted almost entirely to a few divisive issues:

restricting access to abortion and birth control, preventing assisted suicide, and limiting the medical options and protections available to LGBTQ+ people. Because these issues have received a megaphone from the Christian right, the church has, for many people, become a caricature of itself and alienated a huge population of people. Shouldn't the good Samaritan parable (and its corollaries in other faiths) guide our why on health care? How would the world view the church in particular if it heard people of faith express an interest in ensuring access to good-quality health care at fair prices? As we've realized, we can lead with this common why and still reach vastly different conclusions about policy. We can lead with our values about caring for our neighbors without reaching the conclusion that there is only one right way to get there.

Leading with why should influence the how in terms of both the substantive outcomes we advocate and, more importantly, the way we participate in the process. When we lead with the values that inform our faith — compassion, forgiveness, and love — we enter into even the most emotionally charged discussions with a new perspective. We might not change our minds about the outcomes, but we can change our conversations by listening with openness and receptivity to those who think differently than we do. The two of us can change our discourse by expressing our intentions, rather than allowing those intentions to be distorted by partisan assumptions. Leading with why can also change our hearts. We find over and over that defining our values reminds us that political engagement is not the only and certainly not the ultimate vehicle for expressing those values, a subject we'll return to throughout this book.

This philosophy is not confined to people of faith. Simon Sinek's TED Talk on leading with why has been viewed more than thirty-six million times. In it, he explained that inspirational leaders work from a model that he encapsulates as the "golden circle." In the center of the circle is "why." According to Sinek, truly great leaders clearly identify, communicate, and act based on the reason their business or organization exists. "Why" is always propelling "how" and "what." Sinek also noted that "why" should be expressed as a verb:

For values or guiding principles to be truly effective they have to be verbs. It's not "integrity," it's "always do the right thing." It's not "innovation," it's "look at the problem from a different angle." Articulating our values as verbs gives us a clear idea — we have a clear idea of how to act in any situation.[16]

This instruction is helpful in framing any political debate. Whether the motto is "Love thy neighbor" or "Treat others as they want to be treated," we can all tap into a personal value that can guide a more inquisitive, productive discussion about any political topic.

Inquisitive and productive discussions can be the building blocks for a new kind of politics. One of the reasons that we're able to talk to each other, fully aware of our many differences in thought, is that we trust each other's why. We trust that we are both doing our best to love our neighbors. We trust that we both love our country and want to do what is best for the country and all its citizens. We trust each other to care about "the least of these" and to think carefully about what data and research tell us about the effectiveness of different systems. That means we come to a health-care discussion or any other policy discussion trusting that we both want good outcomes for everyone. When we strip away the demonizing intentions, we can move our conversations out of the mud and into terrain that might help us start solving problems.

CONTINUE THE CONVERSATION

We find that leading with why in every aspect of our lives has been transformative. Our whys as people of faith are easily sourced from the commandment to love God with all our hearts, minds, souls, and strength. Our whys as parents — developing people who will be kind, respectful neighbors who think independently and contribute to their communities — inform how we spend our time and how we raise our children. Our whys in marriage — cultivating lifelong, loving relationships with equal partners that make both partners better people — inform how we interact with our spouses. Our whys in a podcast — modeling the conversation about politics we want to see happening in our country and inspiring others to engage in that conversation — guide our editorial and business decisions. Once you tap into "why" as a decision-making tool, you'll never go back.

1. Why do you care about politics? If that question seems too big to answer (and if that's the case, we love it!), take it in

small pieces. Why are you reading this book? Why do you watch or read the news?

2. What values are most important to you? Choose two or three that really define either your faith or your personal ethics. Can you, as Simon Sinek suggests, frame those values as verbs?

3. Choose a policy issue that has been difficult for you to discuss with others. Consider that issue in light of the value statements (your "whys") you just constructed. Are you approaching the issue from your whys? Are you approaching discussions about the issue from your whys? If the answer to either question is no, how might you rethink your approach without rethinking your whys?

CHAPTER FOUR:
PUT POLITICS IN ITS PLACE

Many of us avoid political conversation because of the risk of conflict, the risk of vulnerability, the risk that we'll be challenged and that we might have to change. And those risks are very real. But we have found that it is worth the risk and, in fact, the very personal work we have to do in order to participate in open-hearted political dialogue. Such dialogue is a spiritual exercise, one where we give grace to ourselves and others while facing our own faults, frustrations, and fears. We learned we had to take off our jerseys and stop treating politics like a sport. Once we stepped out of the arena, we realized we were allowing our position on the team to become our one and only value. We had to stop allowing party membership, politicians, and single-policy stances to become the sole representation of our values. We had to ask ourselves hard questions about why we supported certain positions and what fundamental values animated us and connected us to our fellow citizens. But the hard work isn't over yet, and the next step is essential to reach out and engage in conversation with others.

In order to continue moving forward, we have to put politics in its place.

In many ways, we treat politics, and specifically the government, as both the sole cause of all our problems and the sole solution. It has become the one societal institution expected to shoulder every problem facing us. There was a time when many other institutions shared the load, but those institutions have suffered under the weight of the past several decades' tremendous societal changes, and we've turned our hopes and expectations toward the government instead.

It is obvious that most of us are dissatisfied with the current state of many of our institutions. We are frustrated with public school systems, even when we are pleased with our local schools. For more than a decade *Education Next* has polled Americans about their local schools as well as the national public education system. More than half give their local schools high marks, while only a fourth give the same high marks to our public education generally.[1]

We are also dissatisfied with churches, which is reflected in how church attendance continues to plummet. In 1973, Gallup polling ranked organized religion as the most respected institution in America. Forty-three percent of those polled said they had a great deal of confidence in the church. Today, only 20 percent have faith in the church and its role in our national life.[2] We are also dissatisfied and distrustful of our national media. Trust in the media dropped to a historic low in 2016, according to Gallup, with only 32 percent stating that they had trust and confidence in the fourth estate.[3]

Again and again, it is politics we point to as the problem in each institution. The government is either too involved with education or not involved enough. Churches are too political or not political enough, depending on what church you attend and who you ask. The media is merely a mouthpiece of the political establishment, which is either a problem or a source of pride depending on which outlet you're talking about and whether they represent your politics. The word *politics* has also become a catchall for any human interaction we don't enjoy. Ask anyone why they are dissatisfied with their job. Very often you'll hear "office politics" as a response. Church conflict? "Politics."

However, politics is not the only or even most significant force at play in these problems, and government — or an absence of government — cannot be the only solution. Whenever we make one thing the central cause of a problem or the singular solution to that problem, the stakes are always too high to allow honest conversation or vulnerable reflection. So, if we've removed our jerseys and examined our values, we cannot return to a place where politics is the sun around which we all revolve. If we do, we will lose our ability to move forward at all. The state of Congress over the last decade bears this out. We are in political paralysis because we've decided that every issue is existential. This has resulted in the current lack of progress. Our values provide us with gravity, grounding us in principles that are more enduring and more important than even the most compelling political issues of the day.

By elevating politics above everything else, we have also removed agency from our lives. J. D. Vance, in his *New York Times* bestseller *Hillbilly Elegy,* spoke to this directly as he reflected on how people view government in his hometown in Appalachia. He argued that "there is a cultural movement in the white working class to blame problems on society or the government, and that movement gains adherents by the day."[4] He addressed how his own community has lost a sense of agency, both by pinning their problems on the government and still looking to it as the only answer to their problems. He described his own grandmother's views on politics and government:

Mamaw's sentiments occupied wildly different parts of the political spectrum. Depending on her mood, Mamaw was a radical conservative or a European-style social Democrat. Because of this, I initially assumed that Mamaw was an unreformed simpleton and that as soon as she opened her mouth about policy or politics, I might as well close my ears. Yet I quickly realized that in Mamaw's contradictions lay great wisdom. . . . I began to see the world as Mamaw did. I was scared, confused, angry, and heartbroken. I'd blame large businesses for closing up shop and moving overseas, and then I'd wonder if I might have done the same thing. I'd curse our government for not helping enough, and then I'd wonder if, in its attempts to help, it actually made the problem worse.[5]

It is true that government can absolutely make our problems better or worse. Both of us believe passionately in the power of politics to change lives, which is why we dedicate our time to helping people talk about it. However, we also believe that each and every one of us has a role to play in our own lives and in the institutions that are important to us. Each and every one of us can exert influence in small ways in our companies, our churches, our schools, and even the media. By abdicating our authority — and ignoring our responsibilities — in the problems facing our country and our world, we begin to see politicians and politics as the only solution. We become willing to do whatever it takes to achieve our desired outcomes in the political arena, and we do little but complain when policy fails as the sole solution. In order to move forward, though, we have to keep politics in its place and not put everything in that one basket. Legislation is not the answer to every private concern, every religious debate, every problem within the family, our minds, our heads, or our hearts.

We must keep politics in perspective. Our government is important, yes, but we don't have to care about it every minute. Our values are certainly represented in our politics, but politics should never be the only or even the greatest manifestation of our values. Our faith can inform our politics, but we must maintain sufficient space between the two for us to see clearly when we are and are not embodying our faith through our political actions.

When our perspective is clear and we can connect to one another through shared values, we can start having healthy conversation. However, it's important to note that we can push past hard disagreement to places of compromise and problem-solving only if we stand firmly in identities rooted in a humanity and worth that is far beyond the reach of politics. When we put politics in its place, we know a person attacking our politics isn't attacking *us*. Beth's common refrain is "Ultimately, I know I will be okay." Politics cannot be the sole source of our confidence, happiness, or self-worth. A deep well of connection holds us to one another and to the highest parts of ourselves. That connection will feed us, even in the harshest political climates.

We do not mean to imply that political issues are unimportant. For many of us, policy affecting health insurance or military engagement or gun control can be the difference between life and death, and we get that. But what we are saying is that as a nation we have made political issues philosophical quicksand in which all of us are drowning. We can resurface by understanding that political issues are one expression of our values, but not the only expression.

One way we tend to assign politics too much status or power is by artificially heightening political stakes with the notion of a slippery slope. We bind ideas together that aren't as inevitably connected as we think, leaving no space for judgment, movement, or evolution in how things work. While it's important to identify the ripple effects of any policy and to prepare for the consequences, too often what happens is a collective adoption of slippery-slope reasoning and an abandonment of logic altogether.

To put it in the kind of terms we've tried not to think about since we took the LSAT, the slippery slope takes the form "if A, then, through a series of steps, Z. Z is unthinkable, so A is bad." It's not wrong to ask questions about the potential of steps B through Y to land us at Z. We also shouldn't cede control to the universe and behave as though B through Y are predestined to occur. But that's precisely what we do in nearly all our political beliefs: create scenarios where A means Z is inevitable. And our Z is nearly always some version of "I am being coerced against my will and beliefs, our democracy is shattered, and hope is lost."

You've probably encountered this in conversations with friends on both sides of the aisle. Sarah has had Facebook arguments about gun violence that inevitably prompt someone to say that any regulation of gun purchases will result in us losing our constitutionally guaranteed right to bear arms. Beth has tried to explain how frustrating, costly, and sometimes damaging well-intended employment laws are for businesses, only to hear that without such regulations, we'll usher in a second Jim Crow era. We're all guilty of assuming that a step in a direction we don't embrace or understand will lead to extremes.

This is our pattern. We struggle to meet people we disagree with in healthy conversation. Our brains take shortcuts that help us protect ourselves, which, politically, means that any step in a direction we don't embrace or understand is completely threatening. When we believe the power to either fix or destroy everything lies in our politics, it becomes increasingly important to label people who disagree with us as enemies and to ensure that our thoughts prevail. We don't want to talk about politics, especially with people who disagree with us, because we've decided our politics define us and everything around us. We're forgetting that rarely is it only one thing that affects the course of our lives and the world. More often there is a complex interplay of personal, structural, cultural, and legislative forces happening, and the world likely won't end because we take a step toward one another to talk.

Take the example of welfare, which we discussed in chapter 2. A person who wants a robust welfare system because they see the need to care for the poor would be foolish to say, "Government support is the only way, so I will never give a dollar to charity." Poverty is a complex problem, and even if you believe the government is an important part of the solution, surely you can acknowledge that it is not the totality of the solution.

We have elevated the importance of government and the stakes behind political issues to the point of believing that every Supreme Court decision and state law will lead to a utopia or dystopia. The reality, though, is that public policy is not the only driver of our behavior. Alcohol is legal, but not everyone drinks. The existence of a legal right to abortion does not mean every woman will have an abortion (just as we know that the prohibition on abortion did not prevent every abortion). The tax code contains incentives for charitable giving, but not everyone gives to charity. In terms of public policy, neither the carrot nor the stick carries a level of influence sufficient to justify the public outcry we see around every issue. This isn't to say that public policy is unimportant. It is to say that we have given it outsized importance, and the results, particularly when it comes to our interpersonal relationships and dialogue, are unproductive and harmful.

We can move to a more productive outlook when we realize that our personal values are not lost if we collectively make decisions that deviate from those values. We can hold on to our values without needing public validation of them. We can recognize that different considerations are at work in the public debate than in our private lives. We can seek out expressions of our values beyond the public sphere. We can recognize that sometimes more good comes out of expressing our values through private action than through public debate.

Our best blend of public and private

responses seems to occur in the wake of real tragedy. Hurricanes, wildfires, and mudslides have become more common and deadlier in the United States in recent years. Our federal and state governments have responded to these tragedies with varying degrees of commitment, resources, and competence. So many people have stepped up to fill the gaps left by federal aid, and the results are remarkable and critical. Writing for *The Atlantic,* David Graham explained that federal and state relief efforts depend on entire communities rising to the challenge.[6] During Hurricane Harvey, the "Cajun Navy" — regular citizens setting out in recreational boats to help their neighbors — served as life-saving first responders. The Cajun Navy is just one of many groups of private citizens who gave time and money to help those in need. Graham went on to explain that the engagement of private citizens in disaster relief is not a failure at the federal level. It is, in fact, a successful use of all resources.

The ethos behind these efforts is straightforward and admirable: *Some people are in trouble, and other people have the tools to help them. Why wouldn't they? . . .* In fact, the expectation that civilians will spring to action is central to the way federal, state, and local governments approach huge disasters like Harvey. There's simply no way for those levels of government to marshal the resources fast enough to do all that needs to get done. Roads are impassable; resources are spread out; and manpower is limited.[7]

Imagine what it would be like if we kept that ethos running through our public discourse. Some people are in trouble, and other people have the tools to help them. What could we do to combat homelessness and addiction if we each saw ourselves as a critical resource to our neighbors who are in trouble? What could we do to transform education if parents saw themselves as critical resources to their children's learning and development rather than as consumers of schools? There isn't only help for us "out there" from the government. It is also on us. In fact, in many ways, we are the government. We are the nonprofit world. We are the private sector. We are the resources for our neighbors in trouble. Because politics is so (and often falsely) binary, it makes us believe every situation has two options and we have to choose. The reality is we don't. It's not all government or no government in any situation — especially natural disasters.

Because this reality can be overwhelming, sometimes we use politics as a vehicle to escape our responsibilities and shortcomings. We attach ourselves to an issue and fight the other side with all our might, telling ourselves that this battle of good and evil is our redemption. Look at Westboro Baptist Church, an organization that has sadly failed to put politics in its place. The Westboro leadership has allowed political sentiments to take priority over spiritual truths, and the result is a congregation that protests the funerals of soldiers and regularly engages in hate speech. If this congregation put politics in its place and spent its time, energy, and resources acting out of love to help their neighbors, it could be a radical force for good in the world instead of a symbol of the danger of zealous theology.

Westboro is an extreme example of an ordinary problem. Sarah has experienced a more everyday example of what happens when politics — in this case a single vote — becomes the focal point, even *within* the parties themselves. Months after the 2016 election, Sarah shared on Facebook that she had voted for Senator Rand Paul (a Republican), due to his strong opposition to the continuing authorization of the war on terror. Sarah is an elected official and active member of her local Democratic party, where she serves on the executive committee. Immediately people began calling for her removal from the local party executive committee because she had violated the bylaws stating that a party member could not openly support a candidate from the opposing party. Despite the fact that Sarah did not support Paul during the election (she didn't actually know she was going to vote for him until she was in the voting booth!), and despite her active Democratic service, a single vote for a Republican was too much for many of her Democratic community members to take. A single political decision, in their eyes, overwhelmed all her past work and progressive ideas. She wasn't checking all the boxes, and that was unacceptable. All the past dialogue and work she had done was erased. Instead of putting Sarah's vote for Paul in its place among her several years of membership, members of the party were willing to use this one decision to oust a dedicated elected official. She was no longer a neighbor or a friend or even a complex person. She was wrong, and that was that.

We can find our way back from this less than nuanced approach by first and foremost reminding ourselves that those around us are our neighbors. We have to practice seeing each other as human beings — not walking opinions or ideologies. We also have to remind ourselves that our neighbors are not here for the sole purpose of allowing us to exercise our political opinions or win arguments. Putting politics in its place inside our communities is about reminding ourselves that our communities aren't just about politics. One way to keep ourselves centered on community and service instead of conflict and politics is by gently and regularly posing the question, "How can I personally be of service to my neighbors?" Sometimes politics will help answer that question; more often, it won't. The key is to find our specific work, asking, "What can I do with my two hands, with the gifts that I've been given?" We don't have to find this question threatening or overwhelming. We can just show up each day to do our work in the world, and when we do, the results will blossom.

Dr. Catherine Roma is a beautiful example of showing up each day with individual talents to change the world. Dr. Roma is a choral conductor and musician. She has used music as a vehicle for social good throughout her career. Beth had the privilege of hearing three of Dr. Roma's choirs sing recently. The performances occurred via video because the choir members are incarcerated. Dr. Roma visits local prisons several times a week and leads inmates in song. In 2012, the UMOJA Men's Chorus she formed in the Warren County Correctional Institution in Ohio won two gold medals at the World Choir Games. Dr. Roma is doing much more than inspiring an award-winning chorus: "She makes people not only want to change musically but inwardly as well," choir member Norman Whiteside said. "It goes beyond music."[8]

This may seem like a purely private activity without much link to politics, but we can think of no more important and beautiful contribution to criminal justice reform in the United States than Dr. Roma's work. We will never achieve true reform to sentencing laws until the public begins viewing individuals who have committed crimes as people worthy of grace and redemption. In leading prison choirs, Dr. Roma is doing powerful political work because she is doing it positively from a place of contribution. She's not putting all her hopes in what the government might or might not do; she is putting her hand to the part she can play. Her neighbors are in trouble, and she is choosing to be of service to them.

A key to unlocking the ways in which we, like Dr. Roma, can respond as whole communities to our neighbors and dramatically extend the love that underlies our values is keeping politics in its place. Whatever the source of our individual values, politics should take a back seat to the care we demonstrate for one another. We can work for issues, enthusiastically support candidates, and cast our votes knowing they matter. Simultaneously we can take care of ourselves and each other in the process, finding a sense of peace no matter how the political winds end up blowing.

The 2016 presidential election poignantly illustrated our tendency to think of politics as a life-or-death matter. In the days leading up to the results, commentators explained that after the election, no matter the result, half of the country would wake up feeling like they didn't belong in America anymore. While we viewed the election as important and highly consequential, we never saw it as the beginning or end of the American experiment. On November 6, just days before the election, we posted an entry on our blog titled "There Will Be a Wednesday," hoping to encourage our listeners to keep politics in its place. It remains a sum-mary of how we view political stakes.

Elections are important. This election is important. Our political ideas and affiliations are important. How we vote is important.

But none of these things are singularly important. They are important pieces in much larger, richer puzzles. It's important to see those puzzles in their entireties and to intentionally focus on the bigger picture, even and especially as the smaller picture is coming to resolution.

Tuesday is important. There will be a Wednesday.

And Wednesday will be important — perhaps more important than Tuesday in many ways. To prepare for Wednesday, we might decide ahead of time to keep some important truths in mind:

America is bigger than one election.

America is more than its president, control of its Congress, and its judiciary.

Democracy is an agreement that we're all responsible for implementing. Democracy is a fire we're all responsible for tending.

If we want to trust our institutions, we can start by forgiving them.

If we want a president worthy of the office, we can start by supporting that president.

If we want a Congress that works, we can give our representatives space to do that work.

If we want a process of integrity, we can start by respecting the outcome of that process.

We can ask questions without issuing condemnations.

We can seek greater accountability without criminalizing that with which we disagree.

We can improve our process by first seeking to better understand it.

People are complicated. People are more than our candidates of choice. People are more than our ideologies. People believe things for reasons we might not fully understand.

Voting is the easiest exercise of our civic duty. The real work is in paying attention, caring, communicating, and finding the best way to contribute from where we are.

We can be the change we want to see in the world, and that's true no matter who wins.

There will be a Wednesday, and we can choose to make Wednesday a day that we can be proud of.[9]

CONTINUE THE CONVERSATION

Ecclesiastes 3:1–8 famously tells us that "there is a time for everything, and a season for every activity under the heavens." Reading this passage is always comforting because it reinforces God's grace — that sense that everything belongs. What we think and do politically belongs. Our political action has a place. But it is just one piece of a life well lived. It is, in a sense, one activity under the heavens. It is not the totality of our being. Volunteer work also belongs. How we treat our neighbors, how we raise our children, how we study and work belong too. As Solomon wrote, we are here to laugh, dance, mourn, weep, tear, and mend.

Some will read these words and say that we are able to view politics as important, but not everything, because we write from a place of privilege. We do not deny that. It is also true that successful movements to advance civil rights for historically marginalized groups relied not just on political action. Music, culture, art, television, churches, neighborhood groups, and volunteer organizations have played instrumental parts in bringing about change. Again, we aren't saying that politics is trivial. We are saying that politics should not eclipse the rest of our lives.

1. Think about an election that was important to you. How did you feel when your candidate won or lost? Did the results have the impact you predicted?
2. In what ways do you see neighbors in trouble?
3. Choose one way that you see your neighbors in trouble. What talents, resources, or abilities do you have to be of service to them? As you answer, consider the parts of your answer that involve political participation and the parts that do not.

■ ■ ■ ■

PART TWO:
TURN YOUR EYES
OUTWARD

■ ■ ■ ■

CHAPTER FIVE:
GIVE GRACE

We've argued that the first (and perhaps most difficult) step of engaging with others about politics is engaging with ourselves. Thoughtful dialogue has to begin from a place of self-awareness. We've done the hard work of showing up to talk and taking off our jerseys. We've examined our motivations and looked deep within ourselves to see the bigger picture outside politics. Now we move outside ourselves and start thinking about everyone else. We start engaging, and we believe the first step of engagement is giving grace. Our political dialogue is diseased, and we believe this sickness is caused by a grace deficiency.

The mystery of grace has been explored in both religious and secular traditions throughout time. It's difficult to pin down the concept with a simple definition. Many families "say grace" before meals and sleep, with or without reference to a higher power, and that invocation seems to be a way of staying connected to grace as a concept, value, and state of being. When we talk on the podcast about the need for grace in our political discussions, we mean infusing discussions with kindness and respect for no reason other than to uphold the dignity of our fellow humans. We mean extending the same unmerited love that we believe flows from God to even our most strident political adversaries. We mean celebrating our fellow Americans rather than dismissing each other based on party labels, policy positions, and voting records. We mean recognizing the unproven, unverifiable worthiness in every person we encounter. We mean seeing each person as enough, whether or not we agree with them. Frederick Buechner described grace this way: "The grace of God means something like: Here is your life. You might never have been, but you are because the party wouldn't have been complete without you."[1] Imagine the transformative impact of viewing our fellow citizens as though our big, messy country wouldn't be complete without them, as though we all belong here together, as though the challenge of working through a diversity of perspectives is an inherent, beautiful part of the American experience

— of the human experience.

The polarization manifesting in nearly every aspect of our political culture results from a grace deficiency. As is often the case, we cannot extend grace to others because we do not extend it to ourselves. We fail to give ourselves the grace necessary for genuine and effective political participation. We so often hear "my vote doesn't count." Yet races are decided by narrow margins all the time. In November 2017, a race in the Virginia House of Delegates was decided by pulling names from a bowl because the vote was deemed a tie after all the recounts. A single vote decided a school district election between J. Michael Clara and Alama Uluave in Utah in 2004. In 2008, Stephen Wukela defeated incumbent Frank Willis by one vote to win their party's nomination to run for mayor in Florence, South Carolina. Beyond these few examples of many narrow victories, our votes matter because showing up matters. Extending grace to ourselves facilitates belief in our own value and worthiness — that our voices, our choices belong in the system, regardless of outcome. Our participation contributes. The process would not be complete without us. And that includes our participation beyond voting and activism. Individuals with genuine passion for public policy refuse to run for office based on beliefs that they are unqualified or undesirable. What if a small fraction of the people who have thought about seeking office extended themselves grace? What if they believed that despite their shortcomings, they are worthy of participating in our citizen government?

Another symptom of this grace deficiency is the way we speak about politicians. It has become almost cliché to characterize political races as a "lesser of two evils" choice. Too often we view politicians as villainous caricatures instead of as our fellow citizens. Politicians are human beings worthy of our respect. Seeking out public service (and, yes, the accompanying power and opportunities for personal gain) does not make a person less worthy of being treated with kindness than others. The many individuals serving in our local, state, and federal governments often do so at great personal risk and expense. Every aspect of their lives is scrutinized. Their families suffer ridicule. Their children are bullied. They risk physical harm and endure verbal abuse. If we cannot extend the grace required to admit that there are downsides to public service, how can we ever truly motivate people to run with eyes wide open — instead of attracting only those ready to let their egos blind them to the costs?

The largest and most disturbing manifestation of our grace deficiency is the way we treat each other. The hole in our political discourse where grace should reside has been filled by equivocation, bitterness, and derision. We view each other with skepticism: "If you do not agree with me, then your motives are suspect." This skepticism of each other's motives is what concerns us the most. Michael Wear, who directed faith outreach for President Obama's historic 2012 reelection campaign, says we have to believe — especially as people of faith — that we can come to "equally faithful, yet different, conclusions" in politics and in the voting booth.[2] However, we seem incapable of doing that. The other side's motives must always be nefarious. It's not that people on the left have reached a different conclusion on abortion; it's that they want to kill babies. It's not that people on the right believe different things about the social safety net; it's that they hate poor people.

We start to be defined only by our conflict with one another. Think of climate change. Today the idea that all conservatives disbelieve science on climate change is treated as natural law. Yet the Reagan and

George H. W. Bush administrations once sought to make the United States a global leader on climate change. As late as 2008, Republican presidential candidate John McCain ran on a stronger climate change record than his Democratic opponent, Barack Obama. The notion of climate change as exaggerated or fabricated is a relatively recent invention. These ideas have been perpetuated by individuals and organizations with interests in protecting fossil fuel industries and encouraging conflict. Successful advertising has turned what was once a matter of actual science into an emotionally charged, bitterly contested subject.

The conflict itself becomes our identity, and as a result (a) we can't evolve in our own thinking, and (b) it becomes necessary to vilify our opponents. Progressives believe conservatives are stupid, reckless, and greedy. Conservatives believe progressives are alarmist, gullible, and manipulative. As Bob Inglis, a former Republican congressman (who lost a primary because of his stance on climate change) discussed on our podcast, climate change can feel like an issue on which redemption isn't available.[3] And for progressives who feel a present and severe sense of danger about the earth's condition, how can there be any compromise, any sense of balancing today's economic needs with tomorrow's planetary health?

This focus on conflict — as opposed to giving grace to foster connection and fruitful dialogue — has resulted in our unhealthy obsession with equivalency. If everything is defined in contrast to the other side and if conflict is the goal, then every point should have an equal counterpoint. Just ask every cable news show producer. Our media has decided that presenting the news fairly means that every side is equally represented. This creates the impression that every side is equally right (or wrong) as the case may be. Of course, we all know that reality is almost never so easily broken down into two simple sides, much less two sides with equally valid points.

If there are no shared values sourced from our human connection, then everything must be equal. This is why so many people of faith struggle with a growing culture of moral equivalence — the sense that everything is relative and there are no universal truths, the sense that every opinion has equal weight, because no opinions are rooted in something larger than the last debate. When we aren't anchored in our shared humanity, in our sense that we are all Americans, our debate becomes nothing but an endless tug-of-war. We understand that journalists don't want to be the arbiters of universal truths; that's not the job of media, and we wouldn't want it to be. But we've taken a leap from "don't tell me what to believe" to "if someone, anyone, anywhere made a statement on a debate, that statement is as entitled to equal coverage as all other statements about the debate." It is impossible to sort through so much noise, and it is often damaging to view the world as a boundaryless contest of fact, fiction, truth, myth, and supposition.

Grace helps us make difficult conversations less difficult by tapping into the larger shared mystery of human experience. That's all it is. We aren't required to lose ourselves or abandon reason in the process. We don't have to accept the unacceptable in order to maintain our grace. Grace simply means that all people are valuable. It does not mean that all opinions are valid. Grace does not mandate that we treat all sides of an issue as equally meritorious. We've talked on the podcast about how our promise to listeners is "*plenty* of nuance"; that's different from "we will present all sides of every issue, devoting equal time to those sides, and treating those sides as valid." We aren't going to present unsubstantiated conspiracy theories on the podcast simply because some groups of Americans believe them. We aren't going to treat an argument that is wholly unsupported by data as though it is as valid as one backed up by years of information. But we are going to treat everyone at the table with grace. As David Steindl-Rast explained during an interview on *Oprah's SuperSoul Conversations,* we can both have enemies and love those people.[4] We can vehemently oppose the positions espoused by the people across the aisle from us and still respect those people as people.

There are some occasions when we might not welcome someone to our conversation, when we can respect the person but decide that engaging with them isn't healthy for us. More often than not, these are the people who want to burn everything to the ground. Their stated goals are to troll others, to dismantle government, to discredit all media. Beth has received numerous emails along these lines. Some of those emails are threatening, and most accuse us of perpetuating false narratives espoused by the liberal media. In an open response to an individual who called our podcast "irresponsible and dangerous to our nation,"

Beth stated,

> If two women talking politics from the houses in which they raise children, pay taxes, and contribute to their communities as well as they can is "irresponsible and dangerous to our nation," I have to question what kind of nation it is that you're interested in living in. Regardless, we share it with you. So, I'm acknowledging your views, and you can continue to acknowledge mine. Or not. That's the beauty of America.[5]

Grace isn't rolling over or acquiescing to those who have completely different values than we do. It is simply seeing our shared connections and acknowledging each other's human dignity so that we can continue moving forward as a country.

Grace permeates most of our conversations with each other on the podcast — so much so that listeners often don't even recognize our disagreement because it doesn't feel like fighting. Knowing this, we decided one time to experiment with a different format that would bring our differences into sharper relief. By hosting the Great Redhead Debate, we learned that grace is absent from

American politics in large part by format design.[6]

When we first began *Pantsuit Politics*, the primaries were in full swing. It felt as if there was a primary debate every other evening: Bernie vs. Hillary on health care tonight on CNN! A never-ending line of Republicans debating national security tomorrow on Fox News! We decided to make the most of it and began hosting debate "watch parties" on our social media channels. We would each log on to Twitter or Facebook and find our amazing community of listeners ready to express their frustrations with everything from the moderators to the questions asked (or not asked) to the candidates' answers.

It was obvious to us and to our listeners that they (meaning the candidates, campaigns, or cable news, depending on who you asked) were doing this wrong. The debates were shallow and sound-bite driven. They appealed to the lowest common denominator and our basest emotional instincts. So often you could see a candidate waiting to trot out a practiced zinger or joke. You could see moderators practiced in steering away from complicated (and ratings-killing) answers and toward conflicts between the candidates on controversial issues.

We just knew we could do better.

And that is how the Great Redhead Debate was born. We decided we would debate each other, Sarah from the Left versus Beth from the Right, and offer our competing visions for America. One of our devoted listeners, Dante Lima, volunteered to moderate. We took questions from listeners for two weeks. We stuck to the traditional debate structure, with each of us giving opening remarks and answering or responding within a predefined time limit.

Our hearts were in the right place. You could hear our enthusiasm in our opening statements. Sarah spoke to her passion for service and why she's a Democrat. Beth spoke to her private-sector experience and her passion for servant leadership. As we began debating, however, you could start to hear a shift. The first several questions from Dante touched on issues of public education and women in government. We easily found areas of agreement and were able to articulate our positions without unnecessary conflict.

However, as we continued, we began to occupy our predefined roles as a Democrat and a Republican. Beth defended the role of private industry in energy production. Sarah argued for an increased role for the federal government in environmental regulations. We bickered about the power and authority of state and local governments. We danced around our shared interests only to fall back into our conflicts over profit motivation and government corruption.

Slowly but surely you could hear us begin to become skeptical of each other's motives. At this point, we had spent months talking to each other about health care and corporate responsibility and political corruption. Sarah knew that Beth wanted a functioning regulatory system to care for the environment as much as she did. However, as we continued to debate and try to pick apart our policy differences, it became easier and easier to forget that. As the debate went on, we agreed with each other less and less. The animosity and frustration in our voices grew. We began interrupting each other, and you could practically hear us roll our eyes at the other's answer from time to time.

When we go back and listen to the Great Redhead Debate now, all we hear is conflict — where usually our show is driven by our shared connection and an understanding that we will not doubt each other's motives. In the debate, however, the conversation was not the priority. In the debate, it was too easy to stop giving each other the grace found in our shared values and only see the conflict in front of us. In the debate, it was so easy to weaponize our empathy or weaponize our goals to show once and for all that "our side" was the one on the side of right and good. For a certain segment of our audience, the debate was wonderful. They loved the conflict between our two approaches laid bare. There was also a steady stream of listeners who wanted to debate us over email or social media. They were not interested in ever extending grace to the other side and wanted only our approval in their assessment that they — and only they — were on the side of the righteous.

This is what the traditional conflict-driven approach to politics always does. It places our focus on all the wrong things. It elevates conflict and gives each side an outsized role and each opinion a false equivalency. It becomes too easy to see the other person as someone with flawed arguments and misplaced priorities, instead of one deserving of being treated with dignity despite differing priorities or approaches. We doubt our opponents' motives in big and essential ways. We begin to believe they hate the country or us or children or peace. We begin to believe that we don't share basic human values. We begin to believe that the other side's motives are so bankrupt they are barely human themselves.

In the end, what we realized is that debates aren't problem-solving. They are dramatized events filled with manufactured conflict. We weren't trying to find a solution that would make both sides happy. We were arguing that we were a better choice to solve the problem. And conflict prevents the giving of grace and the prioritizing of connection. We didn't need to reinvent debates or do them right. There is no real way to give grace while trying to score points. We already reinvent debates every episode of our podcast. When we sit down to talk about hard political things, we don't begin with an opening statement about why our intentions are pure and superior. We begin by giving grace, by prioritizing our connection, by looking for our shared values, and by treating each other with kindness.

The Great Redhead Debate was an important learning experience, but it is most likely the last debate you will ever hear on our show. You will hear us disagree. You will hear us push each other. However, you will never hear us start any conversation from opposing sides. That's not conversation. It is artificial, unproductive conflict.

We have disagreed vehemently over the role of government, the motivations of businesses, and the importance of regulations since then. There are perspectives we have that fundamentally conflict with one another. However, we no longer spend our time highlighting those conflicts. We don't begin and end with the conflict as you do when you debate. We begin with grace. We begin by recognizing that we owe each other respect and that we share fundamental values as Americans, Kentuckians, women, mothers, and friends. Instead of doubting each other's motives, we try to dissect our shared goals and find space for compromise or mutually agreed-on approaches.

We have a loyal listener who loved the Great Redhead Debate. Despite being liberal himself, he was always quick to praise Beth for a point well made and generally seemed interested in an exchange of ideas. Like many, he took the election of Donald Trump extremely hard. He was angry and frustrated and ready to doubt the motives of every conservative he knew — including Beth. His emails to us after the election grew increasingly furious. Instead of trying to argue with him, we took to heart the valuable lesson of extending grace. We acknowledged his feelings but did not engage in debate. Over months, we kept checking in. We kept assuring him we knew he was angry and frustrated. Despite his hurtful comments, we continued to give grace. We never doubted his motives. We knew he respected both of us and that the initial impact of the election would lessen with time. We kept going back to grace and offering it up again and again no matter how hard it was.

Eventually the tone of his emails began to change. We didn't focus on our conflicts and instead focused on the connection between us. He responded with frustration and impatience but less anger and skepticism. Bit by bit, he stopped attacking Beth and lashing out in anger. It was not easy, but we were able to give grace instead of engaging in debate.

We have learned from the Great Redhead Debate and our relationship with this listener that when we begin with offering grace, the ways in which we orient our conversations fundamentally change. We begin by offering each other the benefit of the doubt instead of being ready to pounce on the first weakness or illustration of conflict. We begin by prioritizing our shared connection to one another instead of our conflicts. We move forward instead of shutting down.

By extending grace to one another, we find space to recognize our shared values. Let's return to the discussion on climate change. There, grace allows us to reframe the conversation from being a blame-driven conflict to an inclusive, participatory discussion of the future. We want the earth to be habitable for future generations. We want to reduce the number and devastation of natural disasters to the extent possible. We want people to be employed in good jobs that provide high wages and long-term security. We want to enjoy modern conveniences and preserve aspects of our culture that are important to us. All these desires can exist together. Grace allows us to get out of identity mode and into problem-solving mode.

First, we do this by understanding that our policy positions are ideas. They are important and reflective of who we are, but they are not limbs. The best ideas are more like elements. They can be reactive, changed, molded. Second, we have to recognize that other people are as entitled to their ideas as we are to ours. As we did with our listener, we have to meet people where they are without expecting them to move. We aren't the boss of anyone else, and grace shows us that others don't have to comply with our worldview in order to be worthy of sharing our world. Instead of having to agree on specific carbon levels, we can ask each other how we can all better care for our earth. We can talk about clean water, farming, fuel innovation. Coal isn't worth a war; it is worth a series of questions that we can all reasonably answer, whether or not we accept that the planet is getting hotter.

As with every value, offering grace to others allows for growth in ourselves as well. As author Byron Katie said, "I am whatever I believe you to be."[7] Grace means seeing our own decisions and decision-making with a realistic sense of our own flawed impermanence. First and foremost, we have to acknowledge that we simply might have gotten a few things wrong. Confirmation bias is a powerful instinct, but we all know deep down that we aren't going to get every call right. We all misunderstand and misinterpret. We all get things wrong. Our perspectives are limited, and the decisions we base them on don't have to be forever. How can we possibly extend grace to someone else for missteps if we aren't willing to extend it to ourselves? By acknowledging our own flaws, we take the wind out of our sanctimonious sails and force ourselves to see what our real problems might be and where we can offer ourselves grace and understanding.

CONTINUE THE CONVERSATION

Religious traditions frequently discuss the concept of *stewardship.* Beth uses the word *steward* frequently in political conversations. She sees the role of public officials as being good stewards of taxpayer dollars, the rule of law, and public trust. *Steward* connotes serving others with a sense of care and responsibility.

How beautiful to think of ourselves as stewards of God's grace! It is an awesome responsibility to recognize that we are here to care for one another, to embody forgiveness, to uphold one another's dignity. Our political conversations, thoughts, and actions are not exempt from this responsibility, and this moment calls out for us to extend grace to one another.

1. In what relationships in your own life do you recognize a grace deficit? Are there family members or friends whom you have difficulty offering grace to in political discussions?
2. What political figure triggers anger and

frustration in you? What would happen if you offered this person grace — even on a small issue or controversy? How does it feel in that moment to let go and offer grace to that person?

3. How can you offer grace to yourself? Is there an area of policy that intimidates you? How could you explore that area without passing judgment on yourself or your ideas? Can you think of a time you were wrong about a political issue or controversy? Can you give yourself the grace to be wrong sometimes and still feel deserving of a role in the bigger discourse?

CHAPTER SIX:
GET CURIOUS

When we walk in grace, recognizing the inherent value in others, we come to understand that we don't engage in dialogue or participate civically to change other people but rather to better understand them, ourselves, and the ideas we are discussing. It is not possible or desirable to bring everyone to our point of view on every topic. In political conversations, we have to meet people where they are and assume they'll stay there. Once we're clear on that fact, we can go about the work of better understanding them and the issues impacting all of us.

It all comes down to personal growth. How can we stretch our capacity for empathy and understanding through our conversations? What can we learn about ourselves and each other? How much better are we for examining and reexamining others' theories and our own?

Sarah often quotes the television show

Sister Wives (trust us; it's relevant). For those without TLC in their television lineup, *Sister Wives* follows the polygamous Brown family. The family believes that polygamy is a spiritual practice because, as one of the wives said, confronting jealousy and different priorities rubs their rough edges off. Engaging with each other and facing our own insecurities can do that in all manner of scenarios outside polygamy! In that process, we evolve individually, which helps us evolve collectively.

Transformative conversation — the kind of conversation that can break open Washington's gridlock and open up a world of political possibility — requires personal humility in the form of genuine curiosity. Seeking out facts, valuing data and expertise, and relentlessly asking questions — all questions: questions about one another's lives, questions about our perspectives both shared and unique, questions about our philosophies, why-are-we-here kinds of questions — these are pursuits that will help us examine ideas, issues, people, and our own beliefs clearly.

When we take a step back from our stories and assumptions, we can see ourselves and each other more clearly. This takes some brain training! It is easy to hear a casual remark from someone and to build an entire story in our minds about everything that person believes and how it relates to what we believe. Maybe you've heard someone say something like, "What really needs to happen is to bring God back into our schools," and you assumed this person is Republican. Or perhaps you've heard someone say, "While I was at the women's march . . . ," and you assumed this person is a Democrat. From those assumptions about political parties (which don't necessarily follow!), we build stories about positions on everything from guns to education to oil. We are so busy layering each other with baggage that we often don't think about the actual issues we're discussing.

In this way, we've made political tribalism a substitute for curiosity and learning about the issues themselves. A 2013 poll conducted by Hart Research/Public Opinion Strategies for CNBC showed that Americans had stronger opinions about "Obamacare" than the "Affordable Care Act" — the official legislative name of Obamacare.[1] Jimmy Kimmel took to the streets, polling people about whether they prefer one or the other before revealing to the bewildered subjects that these two laws are the same.[2] We're forming hardened opinions on subjects without understanding them. It's not that we are too busy to understand the ins and outs of complex legislation — it's that we are more curious about our party's talking points than about the laws or issues. We're not getting to *why* someone would oppose the Affordable Care Act. We stopped listening when they derisively described it as Obamacare.

There are countless examples of people rendering opinions about each other and political issues with incomplete information, not bothering to ask questions to truly understand the situation. President Obama negotiated the Joint Comprehensive Plan of Action, a complex set of standards on Iranian nuclear proliferation reached after years of negotiations among the United States, other P5+1 members,[3] the European Union, and Iran. Most Americans have a deeply entrenched opinion on "the Iran deal" that became a talking point in the 2016 presidential campaign, but few of us can begin to describe the deal and its impacts. More dishearteningly, it seems we don't care to. We're just interested in who negotiated it and whether they are on our team or not. This tribalism isn't a uniquely American phenomenon. After the United Kingdom's historic Brexit referendum, polls showed that more than a million people who voted to leave the European Union regretted that choice once they fully understood its consequences. The Brexit vote, for those million people, didn't represent a considered choice after curious examination. Both at home and abroad, we are making decisions with lasting consequences without enough information.

We are not engaging with one another. How much better would the polling have been on these issues if every American engaged someone who disagreed with them on the Iran nuclear deal with curiosity, or if every British citizen engaged someone who disagreed with them on Brexit with curiosity? When we engage with curiosity, we better understand the issue from both perspectives. We better understand our opponents' concerns. We better understand ourselves.

Instead of getting curious about each other, we take cheap shots. During the summer of 2002, Sarah spent a week in Washington, DC, attending the American Association of University Women's conference. It was an exciting time spent engaging politically with women from all over the country. While riding the Metro, another young female intern heard Sarah and her friends debating the war on terror. Without so much as learning her name, this woman looked at Sarah after Sarah expressed her opposition to the war on terror and responded sincerely, "Well, that's because you hate America." It's an exchange Sarah has never forgotten because it is so indicative of our instinct to insult instead of understand. Because we fail to fully investigate what's in front of us, our politics have devolved from a contest of ideas to an arena that is dominated by emotions and reactions.

In the immediate aftermath of 9/11, patriotism was rebranded by half of the country as unquestioning support of American aggression in the world. Meanwhile, the other half of the country mocked President Bush's intellect and impugned vice president Dick Cheney's motivations. We bought one side or the other, leading us to miss the consequences of a massive intelligence failure that led our country into a long, traumatic conflict. We never looked at our reactions with curiosity and a desire to understand why someone could see the post-9/11 world so differently than we did. We just insulted and degraded each other and moved on.

Getting curious allows us to take a moment to listen to what the other person is saying without reacting only to what we are hearing. We saw a great example of this when we discussed a book titled *Being There: Why Prioritizing Motherhood in the First Three Years Matters* by Erica Komisar, a psychoanalyst. The book is based on neurological research showing that babies rely on their mothers to essentially function as their central nervous systems for the first three years of life. Komisar encourages mothers to spend as much time as possible with their children during that period. A Google search of her book shows what a *Wall Street Journal* editorial by James Taranto described well: People on the right love her theory, people on the left hate it, and everyone seems to be missing key aspects of her message.[4] In the Rorschach of Komisar's research, conservatives have latched on to support for traditional family values and gender roles. Liberals have reacted to a perceived threat to feminism and themes that could create a sense of guilt for women. Meanwhile, everyone seems to be missing Komisar's call to action: greater public support for families in the form of longer paid-leave policies and more generous maternity benefits.

We shared our perspective that her research made sense and that it's good to know what the ideal situation is for a baby so that mothers can make fully informed choices. We heard from several listeners that they reacted angrily to our discussion the first time they heard it. But, rather than stay in that initial reaction, these listeners played the podcast again and got curious about our discussion. When they did that, they realized that we were just acknowledging the legitimacy of the research, not personally criticizing any mother's decisions.

It's hard to discuss motherhood because it is such an identity. However, when we get curious, we can shift from the focus on our own perspectives (and our own defensiveness) and think about the other person's. The decisions mothers make about birth, breastfeeding, and whether to work beyond child-raising are intensely personal and are made against a backdrop of cultural messages that seem designed to make all of us feel selfish and inadequate. Our listeners' ability to pause, recognize how their experiences were causing them to hear from a defensive posture, and come back to the discussion is extraordinary and instructive. We can't get to the substance of Komisar's research without first recognizing our stakes in our personal choices and how those stakes color our perspective.

That's the beauty of curiosity. In trying to

understand another person's perspective, it often gives us the space to understand our own more deeply as well.

We also can't have productive dialogue with others without getting curious about what stakes color the other person's perspective. Our stakes aren't always logical, coherent, or rational, and that's okay. The same holds true for other people. We don't need to discount a person's position because of what's influencing it; we just need to acknowledge what's influencing it.

During the 2016 Democratic National Convention, we spent time walking through the convention halls in Philadelphia, visiting tables and exhibit booths. We saw the usual suspects — Planned Parenthood, union representatives, civil rights activists — and then stumbled upon Democrats for Life. We couldn't resist a conversation.

Two twentysomething-year-old men were handing out flyers and awkwardly avoiding the free condoms that Planned Parenthood representatives were distributing. We walked over to take the materials the young men were offering. We asked them to tell us about the organization, and they did. In detail.

"Life begins at conception and is sacred, and we think that Democrats should value life." Their voices attracted attention from other women roaming the convention hall, and a small group started to form around the table. One woman started arguing with the men, who seemed taken aback. Sarah jumped in to explain why the conversation was rapidly becoming so heated: "What I need you to understand is that it is very, very hard as a woman to listen to a man explain what pregnancy means to me. It is very hard to hear a man say that my life is not as important as the life of the person I'm carrying. I cannot hear that from a man."[5]

The looks on their faces made it clear that these two well-intentioned young men had never considered this perspective. We could tell that it seemed entirely unfair to them that their gender entered the conversation at all, and we understand that. Abortion has become one of the most contentious issues in US politics, and the discussion is stuck. We walked away from the Democrats for Life table talking about how both sides of the abortion debate feel that any openness to hearing the other side out will send us down a slippery slope. If we believe that ending a pregnancy is a private family matter, then we worry that any intrusion on that private matter will end all abortion access.

If we believe that ending a pregnancy is a public matter similar to protecting lives of children and adults, then we worry that any access to abortion becomes a crime.

We are not interested in each other, because we're too busy safeguarding our positions. We seem to have forgotten that the slippery slope is a logical fallacy. People's views on abortion (and all other policy issues) consist of layers of life experiences, belief systems, and group affiliation. Peeling back those layers is revelatory. Perhaps we can find common ground that we otherwise thought did not exist. Even when we don't, we can better navigate social issues when we put our defensiveness down and become more interested in each other.

When we started *Pantsuit Politics,* we wanted to talk about issues with curiosity. As we started developing subjects that interested us, we realized how shallow our understanding of many issues was. How could we participate in a nuanced conversation on trade if we knew little about NAFTA and the Trans-Pacific Partnership (TPP)? How could we honestly discuss the conflict between Israelis and Palestinians without understanding the history of the region? We developed a concept we started referring to as "primers" to help us and our listeners prepare for discussion, and that concept opened our eyes to how little most of us know about the topics on which we claim to feel the most passion. This practice revealed for us the power of curiosity.

The hard truth is, too often we engage with issues only in a search for information that will prove our point. We have been as guilty of that as anyone else. In the early days of our podcast, this was quite evident. Sarah was a Democrat, so she knew she supported the social safety net, free trade, war when Democrats thought it was a good idea, and peace when they didn't. Beth was a Republican, so she knew she supported supply-side economics, deregulation, and a hawkish foreign policy.

We toed the party line without doing the research, or at least not well-rounded, deep research. We often engaged with issues as we had our whole lives. We would do research before each episode. However, that research often looked less like research and more like a hunt for information confirming what we already knew. We would read articles from sources we knew would support our points of view. We would read authors and politicians with whom we already agreed. Even if our initial conscious approach wasn't merely to confirm our beliefs, something as simple as a Google search revealed unconscious bias:

"Why we need welfare"
"Supply-side economic successes"
"Benefits of free trade"

However, rehashing what we already believed and ignoring the holes in our own arguments did not lead to a better understanding of a topic. It didn't even lead to particularly interesting conversations. And our wonderful community of listeners was always inspiring us to do more . . . to go deeper.

We realized we needed to engage with policy — not as debaters but as students. We wanted to get curious and understand the history of an issue and how the debate surrounding it had or hadn't changed over time.

The first issue we decided to tackle was trade policy. It was in the spring of 2016, and the Democratic primary candidates secretary Hillary Clinton and senator Bernie Sanders were locked in a heated battle for the nomination, with the Trans-Pacific Partnership quickly becoming a flashpoint of debate. The Republican primary was also seeing the issue of trade increase in importance as Donald Trump insisted Americans had gotten a raw deal.

We had to acknowledge that we both felt drawn into the debate, but didn't really know much about the TPP or other international trade deals. We knew the party lines, but we didn't know the history or the shifting economic landscape. We decided there was value in engaging with this issue as if there were a blank sheet of paper in front of us: How did these deals begin? How were they received by both parties at the time? What has changed since the debate first began? We wanted to look hard at how things were — not only how we wanted them to be.

By resetting and looking at the issue with fresh eyes, we were hoping to see the issue more clearly — not through the lens of partisan politics. Both of us had engaged with this issue for the first time decades earlier as young women with a desire to prove our partisan devotion. We wanted to leave all that aside and find out if we could see the issue differently with an older (and hopefully wiser) perspective. As we began to open ourselves up and get curious, we recognized that impermanence is not a bad thing. Our support for any particular issue is not signed in blood and need not feel like a permanent commitment.

Most importantly, in order to get curious about each other, we had to have a baseline agreement on the reality of the situation. Reaching that agreement is the first step of the primers. So, in our primer on trade, Beth defined imports, exports, trade deficits, and other types of trade restrictions. With this primer and other primers in the beginning of this series, we realized just how little we knew. Sometimes adding a level of knowledge confirmed how we felt about an issue. Other times it helped us see how little our opinions were based on and how we needed to look again at what we thought.

With the issue of trade, the primer helped us and our listeners see that reality was much more complex than we were acknowledging. Global trade policy and its impact on America's economy and foreign policy cannot be easily broken down into one side or another. In fact, the most interesting piece of the 2016 election is how extreme wings of both parties became anti-trade. The mainstream wings of both the Democratic and Republican parties had agreed on a free-trade approach for decades. Both Donald Trump and Bernie Sanders were able to exploit frustrations among huge swaths of the electorate who did not believe free trade had been a boon for every American.

We had to get curious about those voices as well. Getting curious doesn't mean you support a stance. Empathy does not equal endorsement. We both fundamentally disagree with much of the anti-trade rhetoric. We hear in that rhetoric that the world economy is a zero-sum game with winners and losers. We hear those arguing against free trade blaming immigration and China for all of America's problems. We cannot agree. Still, even in the face of disagreement, we began to see the value in understanding the emotion behind that view of the world. For better or worse, getting curious about trade helped us better understand the history of trade and the undercurrent of fear motivating so much of the anti-trade populace. That fear is real. Refusing to see it or empathize with it does not move the conversation forward.

Using primers to get curious allowed us to see the opposition more clearly. It also exposed the flaws in our reasoning. We realized that the idea of free trade and globalization as an economic engine was more controversial than we thought. Experts on both sides of the aisle do not agree on the long-term (or short-term) benefits of NAFTA or the TPP. It also called into question some of our assumptions about the pragmatism and wisdom of chasing constant economic growth.

When we got curious, free trade stopped being something we barely understood but fully supported. It became one more example of our flawed and dated approach to politics that left so many of us frustrated and disconnected.

Learning about something from the ground up. Approaching a subject as a curious explorer and not a dedicated disciple. It was a completely new way to engage with subjects. It was a completely new way to see the world. It was freeing to shake off partisan ideologies and old understandings. Suddenly every subject became an opportunity to pull out a fresh piece of paper and get curious. We have produced primers on subjects ranging from Cuba to the Affordable Care Act, from immigration to Israel. Every time, we learn history we didn't know. Every time, we understand the emotions fueling both sides of the debate on a deeper level. Every time, we realize the flaws in our own opinions and the ways in which the debate is premised on a dated understanding of the world.

Getting curious allows us to stay connected. We don't have to disconnect for fear of encountering something that might challenge us or illuminate our errors, because winning is no longer the name of the game. Curiosity is an inherently connecting motivator. By getting curious, you are stretching. You are reaching out for information and understanding. It no longer matters if the foundation you were standing on gets rocked, because you've moved forward toward learning, toward others, toward a deeper understanding of yourself and the world.

CONTINUE THE CONVERSATION

It's not only interesting and enjoyable to spend time diving into issues; it's also a spiritual exercise. We think about 2 Timothy 2:15, encouraging us to study, presenting ourselves to God as people who have worked hard to discern truth. Learning is much more righteous than being righteous with an empty opinion!

Primers have been an essential part of our own attempt to get curious. Now it is time for you to get in on the fun. Write your own primer. Start with a blank sheet of paper and learn all you can. This can be as easy or as hard as you want it to be. You could start with an issue or country about which you know very little and are unhindered by strong opinions. Or — if you're further along in your practice — you could try something a bit more advanced. Pick an issue you are passionate about. Pick an issue that feels connected to your identity. Pick an issue fueled by your spirituality. Now write a primer for someone who knows almost nothing about it. Pretend an alien race has landed, and you have to start from the beginning to explain this issue to them. Explain the history, the different stakeholders, and how the issue has changed over time. See where your curiosity takes you.

1. What is a perspective you struggle to understand? Where can you find a little corner of curiosity to explore in this issue or point of view?

2. Think back to a time someone seemed sincerely curious about your point of view. What questions did they ask you? How much time did they spend talking? How much time did they spend listening? How did their curiosity make you *feel*?

3. This one is a little bit selfish, and we appreciate your indulgence. Make a list

of subjects or countries or issues that you would like to see primers on and send them to beth@pantsuitpolitics show.com.

CHAPTER SEVEN:
EMBRACE THE PARADOX

The inescapable conclusion of curious, openhearted dialogue on politics is that conflicting opinions and data can and do exist simultaneously. When we get curious and learn about issues or people or countries from the ground up, we inevitably encounter information that seems contradictory, and it becomes difficult if not impossible to sort it in a way that only confirms what we already believe. Instead we find a universe of complexity.

Despite the presence of complexity, we live in a world that values simplicity. As soon as we are old enough to pick our favorite Disney movie and watch it on repeat, we are fed a steady diet of simple conclusions, of believing people always fall into one of two groups: flawed but lovable heroes or fundamentally evil villains. The stories are not filled with complex human beings. No one asks if Ursula maybe had some legitimate grievances or if the Wicked Witch had good qualities (well . . . not until *Wicked* provided us with the delightful backstory). Questions only complicate something that is supposed to be simple: the diametrically opposed sides of a binary understanding of the world. Right vs. wrong. Good vs. evil.

We wonder why kids can be so cruel when we watch them interact with one another, but we forget that we have taught them (as we were taught) that the world organizes itself in a "you're either for us or against us" way. As parents, we struggle constantly against our instincts to simplify and separate things for our own kids. It's hard to look at your child and say, "I don't know" or "It's complicated." We want to assure them that the world is fundamentally good and we can keep them safe from everything bad. And, if we're honest, we want the same for ourselves.

We try to convince ourselves that we see beyond black and white, but we seem to just search for more complex ways of being right and wrong. We add smaller lines of measurements along the spectrum, and we recognize new gradients of gray. However, we still operate in a world where there are fundamentally two options: true or false, right or wrong, left or right.

The problem is in that little word connecting these debates: *or.*

This *or* that. There are two choices, and you *have* to pick one. You can either be a Democrat *or* a Republican. A liberal *or* a conservative. How often do you turn on CNN and see the anchor placed squarely between two talking heads arguing with each other? We never see a person arguing that they agree with points being made on both sides of the aisle. In fact, using the aisle as a metaphor again illustrates our desire to formulate everything as a linear debate. Our winner-take-all elections also support the idea that there are only winners *or* losers in politics. Rarely do we talk about the groups in which we all coexist together — citizen, voter, American. No, we must pick a side and only one side.

We continue our devotion to this false binary in the way we talk about specific issues. You are either for something *or* against it. (There's that little word again.) We all instinctively look for sides in every debate, and then ask on what side members of our tribe (be it party, denomination, or religion) fall so that we know how to orient ourselves inside the debate. We value purity in our candidates and in our discussions above all else. Not only must you pick a side, but you must commit 100 percent and, without variance, align with that side.

This kind of thinking is not bad. It's a common strategy almost all of us use for understandable reasons. From our first breath, our brains take in an amazingly vast amount of stimuli. As babies, we have no framework with which to process all that stimuli. Even with the addition of language and maturity, the amount of stimuli we absorb, especially in our technological age, is breathtaking. So our brains use simplification and categorization to quickly process the information we take in second by second, doing the best they can with all this input.

This way of processing information means that we make mistakes in our reasoning, and the false dichotomy is a common one. We sort things into two groups — good and bad — and ignore the reality that there could be several hundred categories we're simply ignoring. After all, *of course* there are more options in the American political system than Democrats or Republicans. Simply ask the 42 percent of Americans who identify as Independents (the largest number in the history of public opinion polling).[1]

Refusing to see the truth in both sides or rejecting the premise of sides altogether forces us into corners and harms all of us. That was the point Jon Stewart, longtime host of Comedy Central's *The Daily Show,* made when he famously went on the popular CNN debate show *Crossfire* in 2004 and exclaimed to Paul Begala and Tucker Carlson, "Stop hurting America. . . . I'm here to confront you because we need help from the media and they're hurting us."[2] Stewart went on to harshly critique the two-sided, conflict-driven approach found throughout American politics and the media's coverage of politics. Interestingly enough, years later Begala shared his memory of the extensive conversation he had with Stewart after the show:

> When the show ended, Stewart and his executive producer, Ben Karlin, sat with me and "Crossfire's" executive producer, Sam Feist, for 90 minutes. We had the kind of thoughtful, respectful dialogue that our audience deserved but never got. It has been ten years, and I do not have contemporaneous notes. And, as we have been reminded recently, memory is a tricky and unreliable resource. Still, this is what I remember from our chat:
>
> Stewart thought it was absurd to pretend every issue could be reduced to a forced

choice between the right and the left. I thought that was a good point. Some issues have seven sides, but better to air two than none. Then he said we deliberately booked the show to provoke division. Guilty. A discussion of religion, for example, would feature a debate between, say, the Revs. Jerry Falwell and Al Sharpton, when the truth is most believers fall somewhere in between. His criticism stung because I agreed this was a major shortcoming of our program.[3]

Crossfire was eventually cancelled, but we haven't gotten much better at seeing the world in all its complicated, contradictory, paradoxical glory. This alternative way of seeing things should come easily to people of faith. That God is not the Father *or* the Son but rather the Father, the Son, *and* the Holy Spirit is the paradox of faith. "Both things can be true" has become a mantra for us, and no place is that truer than in Christianity. We are asked to believe both that Jesus was fully human *and* the divine Son of God. We are asked to believe that Mary was both a virgin *and* a mother. One of our most beloved spiritual teachers is Richard Rohr, an American Franciscan friar. In his exploration of paradox in *A New*

Way of Seeing . . . A New Way of Being: Jesus and Paul, he actually listed all the scriptures that embrace seemingly paradoxical statements:

Finding is losing; losing is finding (Luke 17:33).

The poor are rich (Matthew 5:3); the rich are very poor (Mark 10:17–25).

Hunger is satisfaction (Matthew 5:6); satisfaction is emptiness (Luke 12:16–21).

Weeping is bliss; bliss is weeping (Matthew 5:4).

The wise and learned do not understand; mere babes do (Matthew 11:25).

Folly is wisdom; the wise are ignorant (1 Corinthians 1:18–27).

Weakness is strength; strength is weakness (1 Corinthians 1:18–27; 2 Corinthians 12:10, 13:9).[4]

Our faiths can light the way down this third path in which we embrace paradox. Our brains might instinctually categorize in binary ways; however, our journey need not end there.

Nowhere did we find this truer than during our discussion of abortion — a topic that seems to be the ground zero for combustive forces of religion and politics. We often ask ourselves, does it have to be one thing *or* the other . . . or can we use the word *and* instead? One can value life *and* the autonomy of a woman's body. When we release ourselves from *picking,* we also allow our brains to release their death grip on confirmation bias. Embracing the paradox helps us realize that politics is not a collision of good and evil; it's a painstaking analysis of valid, competing priorities.

When we decided to discuss abortion for the first time in January 2016, we desperately wanted to avoid the traditional binary approach to this controversial subject. First and foremost, when Americans talk about abortion, we assume at the outset that there are two — and only two — sides of the debate. There are people who value life — the *pro-life* side — and there are people who value choice — the *pro-choice* side.

Those are your options; choose accordingly.

If you are a Democrat, you don't really have a choice at all. You *are* pro-choice. If you are Republican, especially if you are a Republican politician, you *are* pro-life. Purity is of the utmost importance in maintaining this debate, so everyone has to sign on to this simplified version.

From this vantage point, the unkind and damaging characterizations of the other side seem to take on a life of their own. We almost compete to see who can villainize the other side the most. After all, if we are the good guys, then we have to have a villain. So, if you are pro-choice, the other side hates women. They want to control our bodies, force us to have babies, and create *The Handmaid's Tale* here in America, complete with the funny hats, red robes, and cattle prods. If you are pro-life, the other side hates babies. They want to kill babies and spread death across America and use abortion to help maintain their sex-craved lifestyles full of orgies and forty-week abortions.

Even if we *know* those characterizations are inaccurate at best and cruel at worst, we still seem to accept that these are the rules of the debate. You have to be pro-life or pro-choice. You have to *know* when life begins and be ready to defend that position with science, Scripture, or both. You have to believe we are debating one of two things — the government making abortion legal or the government making abortion illegal. This debate is always framed as a forced binary. It's difficult to participate in the public debate if you don't see it so starkly.

There also seems to be an assumption that fuels the fire of this already reductive debate. In so many other areas, we are willing to accept that we all bring our diverse perspectives and experiences to a discussion and that objectivity — while a worthy goal — is something strived for but never quite achieved. However, when debating abortion, both sides seem to lose all sense of subjectivity. We aren't debating the way we *see* abortion. We are debating the way things *are.* We use science or Scripture to argue that our side — and only our side — understands the objective reality of the situation. Of course life begins at conception. Or of course abortion is a medical procedure and nothing more. The only time we do accept personal perspectives is when we use them to bludgeon the other side with proof that *our* side gets it. We pass around stories of the abortion provider who had a change of heart or the *pregnant* abortion provider who passionately believes in choice. We post the story of the woman who desperately regrets her abortion and now marches with the pro-life movement, or we share the story of the woman who desperately needed her abortion to escape rape or domestic abuse or even death itself.

This flattens the debate into a simplistic argument between two sides: people who value life because it begins at conception and want to make abortion illegal *or* people who value women because life begins at viability and want to keep abortion legal. We miss (or totally avoid) a fuller picture of the world in which we live and in which we are having this conversation. We avoid the reality that sometimes we are talking about very different things. Sometimes we are talking about religion and ethics. Sometimes we are talking about laws and legislation and policy. Sometimes we're trying to talk about both at the same time, which is doable but difficult. Because so often this debate revolves around the intersection of science and religion (throw in government, and you can see why painting this debate in broad strokes seems foolhardy), we often think about this quote from Krista Tippett, host of the podcast *On Being:* "And it's not so much true, as our cultural debates presume, that science and religion reach contradictory answers to the same particular questions of human life. Far more often, they simply ask different kinds of questions altogether, probing and illuminating in ways neither could alone."[5]

■ ■ ■ ■

We started out trying to embrace the complex and contradictory nature of this debate by allowing and authentically sharing our own subjective experiences. Sarah, in particular, has extensive experience in the reproductive community that informs her opinions on the subject. After college, Sarah's first job was running the emergency contraceptive hotline for Planned Parenthood of Central North Carolina. At the time, emergency contraception was available only with a prescription, and PPCNC had a hotline that women could call to easily get a prescription. Sarah likes to say she prevented more abortions in that year than most people will in their entire lives. This Planned Parenthood also provided abortions, and Sarah worked closely with the staff, who dedicated their lives to providing reproductive care to women from all walks of life.

Since Sarah grew up in the Southern Baptist Church, working at a Planned Parenthood was a pretty strong departure from the lessons she learned about abortion as a child. However, from her time at Transylvania University as a women's studies minor, and through her own experiences as a mother herself, Sarah has grown passionate about the importance of trusting women to make decisions for their own lives. Sharing that passion doesn't mean Sarah is unwilling to engage in debate about abortion, as some of her closest friends are devout pro-life Catholics. It only means that understanding one anothers' perspectives can help us create space for connection through shared experiences and values.

Beth also shared her personal journey on the issue, including being raised in a religious environment that only presented one side as an option. Abortion was not discussed often in her church. It was simply understood that abortion was wrong, but Beth was fortunate to be surrounded with loving, open-minded adults. The one Sunday school lesson she remembers on abortion centered on the duty of Christians to support people who have gone through traumatic decisions and experiences. Beth approaches the abortion discussion less as a theological question and more as a question about the power of government over individuals. Because there are so many questions about when and why a woman might need an abortion, Beth feels that abortion is a private matter. In many circumstances, Beth believes that abortion might be an ethically wrong choice, but she sees that (like many other sins) as between the people involved and the God of their understanding, rather than as a decision in which the general public has a say.

Our perspectives on this issue overlap considerably. However, instead of using that opportunity to reinforce why we are "right," we decided to engage with the ways in which we identify and understand the values represented by both sides of the abortion debate. From the outset, we rejected the false choice of either valuing life or valuing women. We embraced the paradox, because as women, as mothers, as people of faith, and as human beings, we value both.

When we let go of that false choice, we were able to look for how our values intersect and weave themselves throughout this debate and how they can appear in both congruent and competing ways on a variety of topics. We tried to separate the two discussions Americans force together: (1) the pragmatic reality of policy in which we must find a compromise and a solution and (2) the philosophical conversation about where life begins.

On the philosophical point, Sarah spoke of her journey of faith and how she became more and more comfortable saying, "I just don't know the answer to that question." Beth acknowledged the importance of spiritual values and also emphasized the essential predominance of legislative values when talking about the role of government. When we made space for both the philosophical and legislative debates to coexist without the emphasis on a winner, our discussion expanded. Most importantly, we stopped fighting about where we are and where we had been and instead started talking about a path forward.

We talked about how we value women and how we value life with regard to pregnancy and childbirth. We talked about how we could better support mothers and stop saying, "All that matters is a healthy baby." We talked about how our culture talks about sex and sexuality and how sex education could better represent our shared societal values both of life and personal decision-making.

It was the first of many discussions of abortion and reproductive rights on the podcast and many conversations that we've had with each other and our listeners. We've spoken with people who sincerely believe that all abortion must be illegal in order to protect life's sanctity, and we've talked with people who believe there should be no restrictions on abortion in any context. We've tested our own views many times over, especially when thinking about the number of abortions that occur because of medical testing. We aren't asking you or anyone else to change your values on this admittedly charged topic. We are just asking you and ourselves and all our conversation partners to hold on to the tension around life and birth. Whether we are discussing policy goals or philosophical ideas, let's allow space for the ways in which this difficult issue can seem to point to contradictory and competing truths. Let's allow space for paradox.

In February 2017 Sarah spoke with Dr. Tamara Mann Tweel, director of strategic development for Hillel International's Office of Innovation and a professor in the Freedom and Citizenship program at Columbia University.[6] In a 2012 Huffington Post piece titled "Heartbeat: My Involuntary Miscarriage and 'Voluntary Abortion' in Ohio," Tamara shared how her involuntary miscarriage had led to a traumatic interaction with Ohio abortion law.[7] In that piece, Dr. Tweel wrote about learning at thirteen weeks of pregnancy that her fetus was not viable. That discovery, and the attendant need to terminate her pregnancy, forced her to jump through hoop after hoop with her insurance company and the hospital to obtain an abortion. She recounted a particularly hard conversation with her doctor's office:

I thought the political nightmare was over. I thought I could start the process of mourning. I was wrong.

Another phone call, this time from the office of the OBGYN performing the procedure. You must come in 24 hours in advance. "Why?" "To sign a consent form." "What consent form?" Silence. "Well, you only don't have to sign it if you were raped." I was still completely confused. "I wasn't raped. I don't understand. What are you talking about?" "You are having an optional abortion right?" "No. I am having a therapeutic D&C (dilation and curettage operation to remove the fetus and womb lining) to remove a non-viable fetus." "But the baby is alive?" "Well, according to my religious faith, that is not so." "Is there a heartbeat?" "Yes." "Then, I am sorry to say, you are having an elective abortion and you must sign an informed consent 24 hours before the operation."[8]

After writing about her experience, Tamara was asked to testify before the Ohio state legislature about a proposed heartbeat bill, which would ban an abortion once the fetus has a detected heartbeat. She testified openly about her concerns about the legislation and her experience with already restrictive abortion legislation. The legislation subsequently passed and was vetoed by Governor Kasich.

Sarah also lost a pregnancy in the second trimester. Her fetus had already passed away, so she was not forced to go through the administrative nightmare Tamara was. However, she also had to advocate strongly for herself to get a D&E procedure instead of delivering her fetus, which her first doctor presented as her sole option. Sarah and Tamara discussed this painful topic from a place of shared experience and values. Nothing was lost by acknowledging that they both wanted their pregnancies, and they both wanted the ability to make decisions about when and how to terminate those pregnancies.

Because we began from a place of trusting one another's motives, we could explore in a much deeper way the paradoxes involved in this difficult issue. Tamara spoke in detail about reaching out to the religious leaders in her own life to help her understand what she should do when her fetus's heart was still beating *and* the doctor was telling her the fetus was not compatible with life.

Instead of seeing the issue as a binary, they encouraged her to see life as a spectrum.

> I called my rabbi. I wasn't sure how I should define life. . . . The way it was explained to me — and I'm not a rabbi — but that Jewish law really does see a continuum between potential life and actual life. But to understand something as actual life it does have to be able to breathe outside of the womb. There is a real emphasis placed on viability. So the fact that my fetus was nonviable meant for my religious leaders that I should have the D&C immediately and I should not consider it a life.[9]

This ability to see life itself in a more complex way opened up for Tamara a new way of thinking about the legislative debate as well.

As she said, "Moral simplicity isn't a fair approach." When Sarah and Tamara began talking in a deeper and more complex way, they were able to discuss all the different moral and ethical concerns and how a wider discussion that distinguishes between life, personhood, and citizenship might be a helpful direction to take the conversation.

Tamara also shared that she felt that respect for each individual's moral complexity was missing from the legislative discussion she participated in while in Ohio. "What does it look like to really respect women going through this and assume that they are moral, ethical human beings *first*? That's what really bothered me. I felt like the state had made all these assumptions about my character, and that they didn't assume the best of me."

Perhaps this is the paradox we must embrace in all areas of political and moral debate. People can be moral and ethical beings who simultaneously reach decisions we ourselves might find immoral or unethical.

There is nothing easy about holding space for that idea, but the alternative seems to be rejecting our fellow human beings' moral and ethical identities. For Sarah, it was Tamara's reflection on how she felt after her testimony that struck her as most profound in a debate about the value of life: "I actually felt like the majority of people on the committee did not respect what I had to go through. They thought that was wrong. They would have preferred that I was just able to get the D&C. Saying that — our side lost . . . and what I realized was that people like me and my case were a sacrifice they were willing to make."[10] By refusing to see the paradox of Tamara's situation, they accepted that a choice had to be made, and making women's lives harder — women like Tamara and Sarah — was a choice they were willing to make.

How different would abortion law look if we embraced the paradox of not knowing where life begins *and* valuing life at the same time? How different would the abortion debate look if we accepted that both "sides" touch on some fundamental truths? Paradox is disorienting at times. It is also empowering. It can be empowering to say "I don't know." It can be empowering to trust the testimonies and experiences of others. As people of faith, we should know that and live that experience.

CONTINUE THE CONVERSATION

We see the effect of *and* instead of *or* in so many aspects of our lives. After all, it would be silly to frame life in the dichotomous terms we frame politics. It's not that we love our children *or* find that they drive us bananas sometimes. It's that we love our children *and* they drive us bananas. It's that we enjoy coffee *and* know that it makes us too jittery to sleep.

These everyday examples help us reach much harder conclusions: "I know you value a woman's choices about her own body, and I think we need to talk about life's sanctity." "I know that trade agreements have harmed manufacturing employment in the United States, and we need to talk about how trade agreements can help promote peace among global powers." "I know we see this issue differently, and our relationship is important to me."

Our faith helps us understand the power of *and* too. Beth's church recently hosted a living Last Supper. After his betrayal of Jesus, the actor portraying Judas left the stage. At the end of the performance, the actors playing Jesus and the disciples administered Communion to the congregation. The entire audience formed a line to receive the bread and cup. At the very end of the line, the actor portraying Judas stood, and he took the bread and the cup from Jesus in a powerful reminder of Christian grace. Judas both made a terrible mistake and remains beloved. Judas is both sinner and child of God, just as we are.

We can hold contradictory, messy, difficult

things together. It just takes practice and faith.

1. How did you first engage with the debate surrounding abortion? How was the debate itself presented to you? Was it presented as simple or complex? One sided or multifaceted? Religious, philosophical, scientific, and/or legislative? How did this inform your opinion?
2. Think about someone whom you know to be a moral and ethical person who holds a political or religious opinion you find immoral. How do you feel when you think about this person?
3. What are some other areas of politics that contain paradoxes? Where are areas we refuse to let two things be true?

CHAPTER EIGHT: GET COMFORTABLE WITH BEING UNCOMFORTABLE

When you actually start becoming open to others in the ways that we described in chapters 5 through 7, it's hard. It's difficult even after you have done the work on yourself that we described in chapters 1 through 4. Nothing about what we're doing with each other or asking others to do is easy. In fact, the point is that it is not. The point is discovering a new reality in which you engage with politics in ways that don't make you feel comfortable, happy, validated, or vindicated.

Citizens tend to approach our political engagement right now as comfort food. We like the macaroni and cheese of hearing someone else parrot our frustration. We like the pizza of mocking people we disagree with, the milkshake of headlines confirming our suspicions. But we need to eat our vegetables. We need to put aside our instincts to retweet that burn or flip on a couple of hours of outrage that we share. We need to do the nourishing, enriching work of exposing ourselves to new and contrary perspectives. We need to build the muscles of learning to understand and be understood by people with whom we don't naturally connect. We will always be dealing with our emotional brains that resist contrary ideas, people with whom we disagree, and information that contradicts our desires, but we can overcome our most base instincts for the health of our country. Choosing to do so is a spiritual practice. We can abide with people and ideas that make us uncomfortable, and we will be better for it.

Somewhere along the way, we decided as a country that we don't want to be uncomfortable at any time, for any reason. We've made that decision at serious expense. More than half of Americans don't have a will, because thinking about death is uncomfortable.[1] We don't like uncomfortable air travel or hotel rooms. We've segregated ourselves into socioeconomically (and often racially) homogeneous neighborhoods because we don't like getting out of our comfort zones. Dr. Sherry Pagoto wrote that we don't exercise because we don't want to be uncomfortable:

Exercise is uncomfortable — uncomfortable *relative to our typical reality,* that is. We live in a society where we keep the indoor temperature adjusted to perfection all year round, wrap ourselves in soft clothing, wear thick-soled shoes to protect our feet from harm, lay on cushy beds draped in poofy covers, and shower and scrub with warm water and soap every single day. Is all of this First-World pampering making us intolerant to even mild physical discomfort? Maybe exercise isn't too *uncomfortable* — maybe our everyday lives are a little *too* comfortable.[2]

We avoid thinking about anything uncomfortable by rushing for something to entertain us. Pema Chödrön, an American Tibetan Buddhist and ordained nun, uses the Tibetan word *dunzie* to refer to "the lifestyle of just flipping through magazines." She said, "We are very threatened by nothing happening, and we are addicted to distractions."[3] She illustrated this unwillingness to be uncomfortable by describing the experience of being on an airplane, where everyone has an electronic device or book or newspaper. What would it be like, she asked, to not have any of those things? Pema suggested that we'd probably all try to go to sleep to avoid actually just being there.

"Just being" is difficult in a country that loves good stories, no ambiguity, and the notion that truth and justice always prevail. Our entertainment choices offer a window into how much we value the resolution of discomfort. Despite competition from a host of genres and the explosion of "new media," procedurals and true crime still dominate most forms of American entertainment. We like to see good guys get bad guys. It might be a meandering, ugly road to justice, but when bad things happen, someone is punished. Writing about *American Vandal* (a Netflix true crime parody) as a "brutal indictment of how the culture codifies and institutionalizes narrative," Amanda Petrusich said:

> We hunger for conclusions, especially when there aren't any good ones. Even the presence of the descriptor "American" in the show's title feels like a subtle gag — a reminder that applying the adjective to almost any noun now imparts instant gravitas, an assurance that whatever is being explored can be slotted into some grand and solemn continuum. There will be meaning.[4]

This need for a relatively simplistic story line that always ends in justice has created unrealistic expectations about our interpersonal relationships and political discourse. To avoid the discomfort of situations with no good options, we dramatize those situations. In our home state of Kentucky, we face a fiscal crisis. There are no happy options, but rather than discussing the fact that any path forward will be painful, we create stories with heroes and villains. Depending on your perspective, we have bloated school administration staffs wasting dollars or a heartless governor who doesn't care about children and the poor or too many lazy people trying to live off the state or people who want to set us back into the dark ages by eliminating critical programs. None of these things are accurate or complete; they just satisfy our brains' desires to make something complex and uncomfortable as simple as possible. We don't like the idea that this problem might not have an answer that feels good. We don't like that there is no one person or group to blame for the problem. We don't like that we can't predict with certainty what will happen when we start adjusting the budget and programs to meet this challenge.

This avoidance of discomfort is a theme

that comes up for us often on *Pantsuit Politics*. As we described in chapter 3, we both decided not to use any pain medication during our births, and we believe that the prevailing American narrative around birth — that it is an unbearably excruciating experience, so "get your epidural in the parking lot!" — is causing negative outcomes and experiences. We understand making decisions that differ from ours, but we think trying to avoid all the discomfort involved in labor (and it's definitely uncomfortable!) deprives us of a fundamental part of being human. We also believe pain is another form of communication during labor. It is a way for the baby to engage with you. Sarah often tells people about the birth of her firstborn son. When she labored on her back it was excruciating; her midwife later revealed the baby's heart rate also tends to drop in that position. We don't believe that's an accident. We don't believe pain or discomfort is ever an accident — it is often a message.

Similarly, we worry that our discomfort with allowing people to die creates unnecessary suffering. We learned from Janice, a listener and hospice nurse in California, that only 41 percent of American patients who are referred for hospice are actually on hospice.[5] The work that hospice organizations throughout the country are doing to facilitate death without pain in an emotionally and spiritually supportive environment is a beautiful model for being willing to just be with the discomfort of death.

What does any of that have to do with politics? When we fear discomfort in our bodies and minds, we lose the sense that, fundamentally, we're okay. We need the security and resilience that accompany our willingness to feel discomfort if we are ever to reach out to our neighbors in the spirit of problem-solving for the greater good. Without that security and resilience, we stay in our corners, which leads to gridlock. It also leads to avoiding and trying to escape every problem that doesn't have an easy solution, a clear hero and villain, and a predictable plot that we know will wrap up shortly. Our avoidance of discomfort is ultimately an avoidance of taking our places in history, and it is the reason that so many problems in American culture and government are spiraling.

Following one of our conversations about birth and death, we heard from our listener, Ashley:

PLEASE. FOR THE SAKE OF EVERY-

THING GOOD (heck, even BAD) PLEASE keep talking about birth, death, and the idea of being uncomfortable and FEELING being okay. And not just okay, but important. I'm not coming from a place that practices this sentiment . . . I'm the one who went into labor and said, "I'm no hero. Give me the drugs." I don't even find it acceptable that I get too hot in the summer. That's how uncomfortable I am with being uncomfortable. But I want to be there with you two. I NEED to be there with you two. We don't just avoid the bad stuff; we avoid feeling good stuff, too. We choose ignorance, we choose indifference, we let other people make decisions. We let other people have the control and then get mad when other people have control! So please keep talking and emphasizing the thoughts and ideas you guys expressed in yesterday's episode. The conversation has me moving toward feeling empowered by the thought of being uncomfortable — mentally and physically — and not afraid of it. Thank you for always keeping me informed, expanding my mind, and making me a better human.[6]

As Ashley said, we don't have to fear discomfort, and getting comfortable with that fact will help us work through some of our hardest problems that lack obvious solutions.

One of the most important challenges of our time is the opioid epidemic in this country. Drug overdoses killed 63,600 Americans in 2016, up 21 percent from the previous year. Opiates accounted for two-thirds of those overdoses.[7] Of those opioid-related deaths, more than 989 occurred in our home state of Kentucky. The epidemic is rampant in northern Kentucky, where Beth lives and where you can see shirts and signs everywhere declaring that "Northern Kentucky Hates Heroin."[8] It hasn't quite made its way to western Kentucky, Sarah's home and where Beth's parents reside. But, as Beth's dad recently said, "It's coming."

Everything about confronting this challenge is uncomfortable. It is uncomfortable to recognize that drug addiction is in or near almost every American's backyard. It's also uncomfortable and necessary to acknowledge that this truth has been present for many communities of color for decades, and that America has reacted differently as the opioid epidemic has claimed the lives of many white Americans. As Jesse Mechanic wrote in "When a Drug Epidemic Hit White

America, Addiction Became a Disease," "The opioid epidemic has, at least recently, been met with empathy, creativity, and heart. The crack epidemic of the 1980s was met with scorn and punishment."[9] We have to live with this discomfort. We can only do better as a culture when we acknowledge where we've failed. Addiction is a tragic example of how America has failed communities of color and must do better. As this epidemic spreads throughout the country, we have to learn from these mistakes.

Living in northern Kentucky, every person Beth knows has been personally and dramatically impacted by opioids. In fact, most who live there are familiar enough with the powerful nasal spray Narcan, and its ability to block the effects of opiates to keep overdosing individuals alive, that they also all have an opinion about its use. It's become so ubiquitous that the Kenton County Detention Center will train any member of the community on how to use it. Even in the midst of suggestions that Narcan is too costly and enables addicts, it is an essential tool for police officers in northern Kentucky and neighboring Cincinnati, Ohio. A local news outlet quoted Chief Tom Synan, who heads the Hamilton County Heroin Task Force in Ohio:

I think Narcan is the only option we have right now. . . . I've been on calls with people who have multiple DUIs and have been in auto accidents. Society didn't tell me or the police officers to let that person die. I've been on multiple runs with the same person on attempted suicides, and society didn't tell me to let them die. In fact, they told me and other officers we should risk our lives to save their life. That's what our job is. . . . When it comes to Narcan, this is a non-issue. People can debate addiction, disease. People can debate if it enables or doesn't enable. To me, this is about saving lives.[10]

It is uncomfortable to recognize the gravity of this situation and perhaps more uncomfortable to talk about its causes. The trouble with opioids is that they are both life giving and life taking at the same time. As a class of drugs, opioids interact with receptors in the brain and throughout the nervous system. They are routinely prescribed as painkillers. While opioids have been prescribed in different forms for centuries to treat pain, the CDC reports that between 1999 and 2014 sales of prescription opioids quadrupled in the United States without an overall change in pain reported by Americans.[11] In 2010 enough opiates were prescribed in America to treat every single adult in this country around the clock for one month.[12] Additionally, opioids are prescribed at a significantly higher rate in southern and midwestern states than in other parts of the country. The CDC says these prescription differences cannot be explained by higher rates of pain.[13]

Last year Sarah was in the audience at a live podcast where one of our favorite medical writers and thinkers, Dr. Atul Gawande, was being interviewed. After being asked about a paper he had published discussing the medical community's role in the opioid epidemic, he clarified and stated very plainly that "we started it."[14] As Gawande explained, medical schools started insisting that doctors take patient complaints about pain more seriously. Palliative care increased, and so did prescription rates. It's important to note that most opioids in the United States are not being purchased from drug dealers. In fact, 27 percent of opiate abusers get the drugs by prescription, and 49 percent get them from friends and family.[15]

Because Americans love to find a bad guy to hold accountable for problems, it would be nice if doctors shouldered this blame alone. The reality is far more complex. Pharmaceutical companies have undoubtedly played a role in creating this crisis, significantly profiting off Americans' pain intolerance and ensuring that opioids are plentiful. Writing for Bloomberg Opinion, Leonid Bershidsky posited that "supply, not despair, caused the opioid epidemic." Citing research by Christopher Ruhm at the University of Virginia, Bershidsky explained that a regression analysis comparing economic conditions to the opioid epidemic is tenuous. He also noted that European countries have experienced similar economic conditions to those in the US, but these countries have fewer opiates and no comparable addiction crisis.[16] A number of states have sued pharmaceutical companies, alleging that the companies fail to adequately warn of the risks of using opiates, that their products are defectively designed because they do not contain safety information, and that they aggressively market their products in deliberately misleading ways.[17]

Pharmaceutical companies have supplied doctors with seemingly endless quantities of drugs, which doctors have overprescribed. Those facts are undeniable. It is also true that American patients have been willing to take opioids in massive and increasing quantities for a variety of reasons. One such reason is access. Health insurance plans willingly pay for opioids but not other ways to treat pain. Access to physical therapy is often limited under health plans, and most insurance won't pay for nonmedical pain management techniques. It's also generally true that Americans expect to live without pain, and that expectation is reinforced by pharmaceutical companies, physicians, and health insurance companies. There is also the "despair scenario" that has been written about prolifically in numerous genres. This scenario generally theorizes that globalization has been destructive to the white working-class psyche, prompting people to escape via drugs.

People in any level of stress are susceptible to addiction. After the birth of her second child, Beth was shocked to find a prescription for Vicodin in her hospital discharge paperwork. Beth had just delivered Ellen in an uncomplicated, completely unmedicated birth. After the birth, she took a regular dose of Motrin and told nurses that she couldn't give them a number on the pain scale because she wasn't in pain. After persistent questions about the scale, she told the nurses, "I mean, I'm uncomfortable. I just gave birth to an almost ten-pound baby.

But I'm not in pain." She left the hospital exactly twenty-four hours after Ellen's birth. Yet, in a discharge folder between pages explaining nursing options and coupons for formulas and diapers, she found a prescription written for her by a doctor who had not treated her. It is not hard to imagine what could have happened had Beth filled that prescription and suffered from postpartum depression or serious pain arising days after the birth.

Several years ago, Sarah experienced intense stomach pain. When she spoke to a doctor about it, the doctor recommended a scan of her gallbladder without any further inquiry into her diet, medications she was taking, or family history. Instead of following the referral instructions, Sarah spent some time price shopping the scan around her area. During that time, she had a conversation with her mother, Lisa. Lisa explained she had had a similar reaction to ibuprofen. Sarah stopped taking ibuprofen, and the stomach pains stopped. By taking a short moment to process and investigate on her own, she saved money and potentially avoided a wholly unnecessary medical procedure. It's hard for us to view our pain as problems we might be able to solve with behavior changes. It's hard for us to view our discomfort as tolerable and within our control. But taking these steps could help (not solve, but help) curb some opioid abuse.

This is the most uncomfortable of truths about opioids: there are numerous causes of the epidemic, and the line between each of us and addiction is exceptionally thin. The Northeast Addictions Treatment Center summed up the complex forces driving the epidemic this way:

The rise of a powerful pharmaceutical industry, combined with changes in the US healthcare system that have left doctors with higher caseloads and increasing fears of medical malpractice, are two of the most powerful factors that got us to the present crisis. Doctors began prescribing more narcotic painkillers (that were aggressively marketed to them) as an easy and fast way to address pain. At the same time, costly medical malpractice lawsuits were on the rise — and their cause could include failing to adequately address pain. Finally, there was an economic downturn that caused job and housing losses, and the number of Americans claiming disability for chronic pain exploded into a perfect storm — today's opioid epidemic.[18]

Talking about any of these problems is uncomfortable. Physicians are understandably defensive, and past that defensiveness often lies a profound sense of "we're the enemy no matter what." Beth has seen a rheumatologist for fibromyalgia since 2007. When she told him that her primary goal was avoiding a lifetime of prescription drug use, he was wonderfully supportive and also confounded. Almost every patient, he told her, just wants a pill that will make it better, and that's not surprising. Sarah likes to tell people about her eighty-two-year-old grandmother who has to convince every nurse taking her medical history that she *really* doesn't take any medications. Most of us don't see doctors expecting to talk about living with an acceptable level of discomfort. We want it to go away, and we want the fix to be easy. We also think more care is better care, as we've talked about before, and care means drugs. We think doctors who can't "fix us" aren't doing their jobs.

Sometimes we don't just want the pain to go away; we need it to go away in order to live. Opioids are used in pervasive, important ways to give people suffering from debilitating pain a reasonable quality of life. As doctors are starting to pull back on opiate prescriptions, we are learning of some devastating effects on people who suffer from insufferable pain. Journalists have reported on patient suicides caused by unbearable physical pain and opiate withdrawal. State legislatures are taking action to restrict opiate prescription, but these restrictions create access issues for rural and economically disadvantaged patients. We can "hate heroin," but we can't banish opiates altogether.

The story of America's opioid epidemic has none of the components that we seem to need. We are eager to place and deflect blame. There are no pure heroes or villains. There are no easy answers, and people are dying in our backyards faster than we can comprehend.

The two of us don't know how to solve the opioid epidemic. We do know that an honest recognition of its causes and effects is necessary. It will require physicians, pharmaceutical companies, lawmakers, community leaders, community members, and all of us as individual parents, friends, and patients to make progress. This is not a war on drugs circa the 1980s. We can't shut off the flow of opiates in our communities through tougher laws or cracking down on dealers (which didn't work with other forms of drugs either!). We are going to have to reckon with forces of industry, medicine, and culture that have led us here and find our way out. We are going to have to examine individual circumstances and be mindful of institutional contributions. It will be a long, arduous road.

We are advocating in this book, just as we do on our podcast, for us to consider accepting a greater level of discomfort in our bodies and in our culture. Regular exercise has taught both of us to be comfortable being uncomfortable. When we move our bodies into positions that require a new level of flexibility or strength, we experience discomfort. But it is the discomfort that creates healing in the body. It is the discomfort that facilitates growth of our strength and flexibility. Discomfort is different from pain. When we experience pain (pinching, burning, pulling), we are no longer working with our bodies but against them. Pain tells us to stop touching the hot stove, but discomfort tells us that we're stretching a muscle just enough to create strength.

These principles directly translate to our relationships, emotions, and spiritual practices. The willingness to be uncomfortable in a marriage creates new depth in the relationship. Practicing healthy conflict is essential to the growth and survival of a marriage. It also models essential skills for our children. Writing for the *New York Times,* Adam Grant described the necessity of conflict to overcome groupthink, to lead to innovation, to achieve scientific break-throughs, and to preserve our democracy in courts of law and the halls of Congress. He stated that parents need to exercise the skills of passionate argument without personal at-tacks for the sake of their kids:

We can also help by having disagree-ments openly in front of our kids. Most parents hide their conflicts: They want to present a united front, and they don't want kids to worry. But when parents disagree with each other, kids learn to think for themselves. They discover that no author-ity has a monopoly on truth. They become more tolerant of ambiguity. Rather than conforming to others' opinions, they come to rely on their own independent judg-ment.[19]

Sarah tries to model this in her home with her husband. When her son Griffin was around the age of eight, he saw Sarah and Nicholas arguing before bedtime. The next morning, Sarah realized that Griffin didn't see the most important part of the interaction, so she took him aside and explained, "You saw us fighting, and you went to bed. What you didn't see is that we worked through it. I want you to know that we worked it out. We had this argument. We still love each other."

Not fighting in front of our children sets up unrealistic expectations. When we can argue without exhibiting anger and yelling, displaying loving disagreement, we teach our children that we love them even when they've done something wrong. We model good disagreement in front of them, and we also exercise this kind of loving conflict with them. As Beth tells her daughters, Jane and Ellen, all the time, "I love you. And you have made a decision that has a consequence." Being comfortable with the discomfort of having to hold our children accountable causes us to grow as parents. It teaches our children how to respect boundaries, which eventually enables our children to set and enforce their own boundaries.

We all grow through the discomfort of emotions like grief, rage, and sorrow, but first we have to allow ourselves to feel those emotions. As Tara Brach has said, "There is only one good question: What are you unwilling to feel?"[20] Too often we try to avoid emotions. We use food, shopping, sex, alcohol — anything to put distance between ourselves and the things that cause us the most discomfort. When we disconnect from ourselves in this way, it automatically disconnects us from other people, and that disconnection becomes a loop of loneliness and resentment.

Those moments of emotional anguish often lead us to crises of faith. While it is comfortable to recite platitudes in difficult times — "God never closes a door without opening a window" or "God puts us on our backs so that we can look up" — it is rarely helpful. We are meant sometimes to do the uncomfortable work of challenging our faith and our understanding of God. In our experience, challenging our faith almost always strengthens that faith. We have to be willing to evolve and transform our concept of God, which is oftentimes based on faulty cultural assumptions rather than Scripture, in order for faith to stand the tests of our lives. We've both worked through these questions at many points in our lives and will continue to do so. Sarah has been immensely comforted by the book *When Bad Things Happen to Good People*. As a survivor of a school shooting, Sarah has found Rabbi Harold S. Kushner's words to be a powerful reminder of spiritual growth through the discomfort of tragedy:

> I no longer hold God responsible for illnesses, accidents, and natural disasters, because I realize that I gain little and I lose so much when I blame God for those things. I can worship a God who hates suffering but cannot eliminate it, more easily than I can worship a God who chooses to make children suffer and die, for whatever exalted reason. . . . The painful things that happen to us are not punishments for our misbehavior, nor are they in any way part of some grand design on God's part. Because the tragedy is not God's will, we need not feel hurt or betrayed by God when tragedy strikes. We can turn to Him for help in overcoming it, precisely because we can tell ourselves that God is as outraged by it as we are.[21]

Sarah has realized that God is the only complete witness to our pain, and the only place to fully expose raw anger and devastation is in prayer (and good therapy). Your spiritual practice might lead you to a different conclusion. The point is that working with our most difficult emotions and questions moves us toward greater maturity, wisdom, and peace.

There is a perfect political parallel. We grow when our ideas about policy and problems are challenged. We become better thinkers, more articulate speakers, and more earnest listeners through the daily discomfort of engaging with other people about difficult subjects. Conflict is healthy. Conflict is necessary. Without conflict we stay in a state of comfortable arrested development.

Discomfort is the path to growth; pain is a sign from the body that we need to disengage. When you are in a political discussion that violates your basic human dignity, you need to disengage. We are not asking anyone to tolerate discussion that actually harms them. For us, there are bottom lines in protecting the dignity of people around their race, sexuality, gender identity, and religion that are inviolable.

We have had to communicate this message to listeners who expressed surprise about our reaction to the white supremacy demonstrations that took place in 2017 in Charlottesville, Virginia. Because we represent two different points of view, listeners sometimes expect "both sides" to be traditionally represented on our podcast. So, many listeners expected to hear our sadness and condemnation of the racism on display in Charlottesville alongside a vigorous defense of the white supremacists' right to protest. We disappointed them. In a blog post, Beth explained our decision to avoid the freedom of speech conversation:

We are receiving messages and comments about the First Amendment in relation to our Charlottesville discussion. They're fair questions and comments.

Here's what I want to quickly share with y'all, in the spirit of love and transparency:

- I believe in the First Amendment. I believe in the right of people to peacefully express even the views I find most repugnant.
- I believe that culturally and civically and then judicially we need to have a conversation about what "incitement" to violence means.
- I also believe that just because you can speak, it doesn't mean you should. Do Nazis and Klan members and white supremacists have the right to assemble at confederate monuments? Yes, unless and until that assembly crosses the incitement line. However, politicians, businesses, and those of us who fervently oppose them should

condemn them for doing so.

- I think it is beyond past time for conservatives to stop shrugging their shoulders and essentially saying, "That sucks, but First Amendment, right?" And that's my intention. The tepid reaction to Charlottesville by the president was not about the First Amendment. The "but Antifa" reactions are not about the First Amendment. I'm not going to pretend otherwise.
  * Side note: we'll talk about Antifa sometime soon. There are problems there, to be sure. We're not going to do it in a "but Antifa" way. There is, for me, no moral equivalence.
- My constant refrain: You're free to speak. You aren't free to speak without consequences.
- Plenty of people are willing to use their platforms to emphasize freedom of speech and assembly. In this moment, in this instance, I'm not willing to use mine that way. My voice, my work is to say, "That's wrong. That's unacceptable in America in 2017, and our businesses and politicians and families must say so in both words and actions."
- I always feel that we are in relation-

ships with our listeners. I hope that our relationships can withstand disagreements about the issues that we prioritize and the ways that we choose to use our voices. As in all relationships, there are defining topics and moments — bottom lines are critical. For me, a bottom line is to ensure that I never use Pantsuit Politics to intentionally hurt people. I think that meeting the news out of Charlottesville with a lengthy dialogue on the rights of white supremacists would cross that line. I hope you understand.[22]

The last bullet of this blog post is the point of uncomfortable dialogue: we hope our relationships can withstand disagreements.

We know that a hardwired reaction to our comments in this chapter might be, "Well, then everyone needs to stop being so politically correct." We want to both be respectful of that reaction and to challenge it. First, we *have* to settle on a definition of "political correctness," because it has become a catchall phrase that is often used to describe any consideration for other people that pushes us to speak in an unfamiliar way. We think about political correctness as taking

239

care in the language that we use to describe people and ideas that are not intuitive to us. We will happily learn how different people groups want to be described and will adopt those words. This doesn't have to mean we agree with them on various fraught issues, such as gender fluidity, but it does mean we become willing students out of respect for our fellow humans (and for us that means thinking of them as our fellow children of God). We want to show them respect through our language, just as we want to be shown respect through their language. We don't lose anything by taking care with our words. In fact, we gain new relationships, new knowledge, and new methods to express our care and consideration for others.

Sometimes realizing that we were using offensive language stings a little. We heard from a listener, who shared *Pantsuit Politics* with her wife and their friends, that hearing us use the term *homosexual* was jarring. She explained with great precision and kindness that she and many other members of her community prefer other language. It was hard to hear. We felt shame and embarrassment. We were also extremely grateful for her message and took it to heart. Any other reaction, it seems to us, would send the message that we are lazy — or worse, that we prioritize our comfort over the comfort of others. That's not who we want to be in the world.

There is a different pattern of conduct that's often swept into the political-correctness bucket that we do find troubling. It's been well publicized that college campuses have responded to student protests of speakers by revoking speaking invitations. There have been reports and studies finding a significant liberal bias on college campuses as well as initiatives to limit conservative thought on these campuses. We think that institutions of education should be in the business of creating discomfort for students. Learning is a form of growth, and as we're describing throughout this chapter, growth requires discomfort. For the most part, we think universities should engage a wide variety of speakers to come to campus each year. Convocations with speakers from diverse backgrounds were hugely influential in our education, and we hope that other students participate in similarly enriching experiences. Universities, like individuals, have to find the line between discomfort and pain. Sadly, there are individuals who have built careers on disrespecting other people through their language and messages. Speakers who have no mission other than to shock students and deliver propaganda about excluding certain races, ethnicities, and populations from America have no place in education. But speakers who have genuine albeit controversial beliefs, theories, and experiences should be welcomed. Students have every right to protest those speakers, but they should not be "protected" from actual ideas.

Cultural appropriation is sometimes included in conversations about political correctness — especially when it comes to Halloween costumes (can we pause for a moment as a country and recognize the unbelievable luxuries we live in that afford us the time and energy to argue with one another about Halloween costumes? Some perspective is often in order when considering these issues). It can be hard to hear that our costume choices cross a line. We posted an article about cultural appropriation and Moana costumes that sparked the most listener engagement we've ever had on a Facebook post. Our audience engaged in a discussion that made us very proud. That discussion circled around what we believe is the heart of the political correctness conversation: it is important to care enough about one another to ask questions and respect the answers. It's not wrong to embrace and celebrate other cultures. It is wrong to do so in ways that are mocking, cartoonish, or otherwise disrespectful to their heritage. Keeping the question "Could this disrespect someone else?" in mind is a way to love our neighbors. Honoring the answers they share, even when it stings a little, is a way to love our neighbors.

The line between celebration and appropriation is much like the line between discomfort and pain. It's not always obvious. We do not always intend to cross it. And knowing where it is requires real consciousness. We can't offer a formula for when people need painkillers. We can't offer a formula for solving the opioid epidemic. We can't offer a formula for knowing when specific language or behaviors will hurt the people around us, and we can't offer a formula for when engaging in discussions with others so offends your fundamental integrity that you need to disengage. You have to *feel* your way through those things, and some of those experiences will be uncomfortable.

Another concept that helps with the effort of paying attention, despite our discomfort is realizing that we are more than just the voice that constantly talks inside our brains.

As people of faith, we strive to connect to the part of our souls that connects us to God and to every other person on earth, and sometimes the easiest way to do that is acknowledge and release the *other* voice that distracts us from that higher purpose. Some call it sin, some call it evil, some call it ego. But, whatever you call it, we can merely witness that talking voice in the brain that says unhelpful and sometimes mean things like "I'll never be able to let go of this anger" or "I'm too messed up to deserve good things in my life," knowing those are just thoughts, not absolute truths, and those thoughts aren't helpful.

Beth established a practice for this that we talk about often on the podcast. She noticed that the thoughts she frequently had about other drivers during her long commute were neither helpful nor particularly charitable. She decided that instead of reacting to fellow drivers in anger, she would train herself to say "Be careful, friend!" when someone cut her off or otherwise provoked a reaction. We've heard from numerous listeners who adopted this practice and found that it powerfully altered their moods and made them safer drivers. Sarah does something similar in Facebook conversations with friends and constituents. She intentionally takes a beat before responding to an angry or hurtful comment, noting her thoughts and what was and was not helpful, and that beat usually helps her respond with a thoughtful question instead of a quip that meets fire with fire. (She calls it "kindness shaming" — which is perhaps not the most grace-filled name, but it makes her feel better!)

In political discussions, we need a reminder that we won't lose anything if we are wrong about our facts, if the person we're talking with disagrees with us, or if we apologize. This is how we are comfortable with discomfort — we can tap into that sense that we are more than our thoughts and more than our conversations. It's also how we know when we've gone from a healthy conflict that challenges us to stretch and grow into something that violates our fundamental dignity.

We need to remember who we want to be in the world and how we want to participate in uncomfortable discussions. When we're not paying attention to the thoughts we're thinking and the words we're using, we get stuck in the discourse version of fight-or-flight mode. We think this is why perfectly kind people can post incredibly hurtful angry comments online. It's why our Facebook friends will type status updates that are passive aggressive or intentionally hateful, using language and tones they would never use in person. Something about the keyboard disconnects us from that slower, more circumspect way of approaching conversations.

We've both experienced this phenomenon, especially on Twitter, where the pressure is to react quickly and simplistically to every headline and expression of thought. It's so easy to fall into a pattern of seeing a news story or opinion column (and sometimes we fail to differentiate between the two because we're reacting so quickly) and instantly composing a tweet that can be reduced to "Yay!" or "Boo!" Instead, we want to stay conscious enough to read an article before reacting to it, to be open to a wide variety of reactions, and to ask ourselves whether we have anything to say about the article that would add to a healthy discussion of the relevant topic. Staying conscious online means that we don't type things we wouldn't say with our voices to another person seated across from us at the dinner table.

In theory, people in faith communities should have powerful versions of this practice at their disposal. We both love Romans

8:26: "We do not know what we ought to pray for, but the Spirit himself intercedes for us through wordless groans." This verse has provided comfort to us during the most difficult and tragic events in our lives. In a more pragmatic way, it reminds us every day that we don't have to have all the answers. It reminds us that some of life will always be mysterious.

So much of our unwillingness to be uncomfortable comes down to needing to stay in control. If we're too hot or too cold, the perfect temperature is within reach of the nearest thermostat (or closer with apps now controlling our thermostats). We don't even have to deal with the discomfort of the seasons. And we don't push ourselves out of our very narrow thinking about political issues. We don't want to feel that anything happening to us is beyond our control. Being comfortable with discomfort is a release of control. So is faith. It is embracing the paradox that no one controls our lives but us and, meanwhile, nearly everything important has nothing to do with us. So what if we don't have the answers to solve the opioid crisis? It's our responsibility to try.

This consciousness is something that we strive for, and we don't always achieve it. That sentence will probably be true for the duration of our lives. That's okay. The simple way to start being comfortable with discomfort is to commit to kindness. Prioritize being kind over being right. Treat people online as though they are friends. Talk about people who disagree with you politically with the kind of love you show your family members. Remember that you are part of something so much bigger than one election, one vote, and one law. Remember that life isn't happening to provide you the opportunity to write one long Yelp review. We need one another. We belong together. As William Sloane Coffin Jr. said, "The world is too dangerous for anything but truth and too small for anything but love."[23] That's the realization that makes the uncomfortable welcome, and that's the way to start the journey of stepping into it that we'll describe in chapter 9.

CONTINUE THE CONVERSATION

Our faith traditions are filled with stories of discomfort. We imagine that Mary's entire existence was uncomfortable — an unwed pregnant mother, forced to give birth in a stable, navigating a relationship with a man who had to rely on an angel's story about her faithfulness and their lives. The disciples took great personal risk in following Jesus around, bucking religious leaders, living humbly and without earthly power. In many ways, the aspect of the story of Christ that we both find so compelling and relatable is God's choice to experience the discomforts of being human as a sign of his love for us.

Make no mistake; being human is uncomfortable. It's uncomfortable to allow your children to experience adversity in order to teach them resilience. It's uncomfortable to give critical feedback professionally in order to encourage your team's growth. As wonderful as marriage can be, a lifelong committed partnership with another person comes with truckloads of discomfort.

Living in community with other people — people who are also experiencing the discomfort of their bodies, their families, and their faiths — is uncomfortable. We have ideas that test each other. We have vigorous and painful disagreements. Rather than being discouraged, we can recognize our discomfort, ease into it, and share the experience of being human together.

1. What topic of discussion in your life (outside of politics) makes you most uncomfortable? Why? Consider writing down your answer to this question and asking yourself who could help you find

a little more ease with this topic.

2. What topic of discussion in politics makes you most uncomfortable? Why? Write your "why" down in three to five bullet points. Hold on to those bullet points, and revisit them after reading chapter 9.

3. Whether or not you are a person of faith, think about your core values that you started identifying in chapter 4. How might you put those core values to work in resolving the discomfort you feel in political discussions?

CHAPTER NINE:
EXIT THE ECHO CHAMBER

We have now taken the time to examine our own views, engage with curiosity and grace with others, and get comfortable with the often uncomfortable results. If we could continue to engage with politics only on this highly personal and individual level, our work would end here. We spend hours every week exercising these skills with each other. We work through our own limitations and mistaken perceptions. We spend time talking through our shared values and goals. We leave our weekly conversations hopeful and energized.

Then we check the news.

We swipe left on our phones or open Twitter against all our better instincts. We turn on Fox News or turn up NPR, and we're suddenly, jarringly, back in the arena. Everyone is wearing their jerseys, and no one is winning. We've made no secret throughout this book that we feel our media environment is in part to blame for the toxic polarization currently plaguing our country. We don't mean any of this "fake news" nonsense. We mean that the media reinforces all our worst instincts and makes money while doing it. An "us versus them" (or left versus right or Democrat versus Republican) narrative is the easiest story to tell, so they tell it over and over again with abandon. This narrative is also the one most likely to tap all our most tribal instincts and get us clicking, watching, and sharing to drive advertising revenue.

However, ignoring the media is simply not an option for us, and we don't believe it should be for you either. The single question we receive most often is: How do you do it? How do you read the news and talk politics all the time without losing your mind?

Listen, we get it. The news can be depressing. It can be frustrating. It can be infuriating. It can be all three at the same time and then some. We understand the instinct to shut it all out and go tickle the nearest baby until you forget Lester Holt even exists. We also should be honest and admit we have both gone on news fasts when we needed to plug back into the perspective that time with family, friends, or yourself can provide.

Disengaging with the news is not a real solution. There is no way to permanently ignore the news, and we shouldn't want to. Being an informed citizen is part of our sacred duty as participants in our democracy. We *are* our sisters' and brothers' keepers, and we owe it to one another to pay attention and show up.

The solution is not disengaging. It is learning *how* to engage with the news in a smart and thoughtful way. Many of us live inside news echo chambers populated by sources that are not credible and that are sometimes manipulative. We learned during the 2016 election that foreign powers were easily able to convince Americans that phony accounts distributing false stories were as credible as the *Wall Street Journal* or *Washington Post.* Being in an echo chamber is not a character flaw. It's a systemic problem. According to the Pew Research Center, almost two-thirds of us get our news from social media. The survey found that 67 percent of American adults were "somewhat" reliant on social media platforms for their news.[1]

As even the least tech-savvy among us are beginning to understand, social media platforms' technology is built on algorithms. Computers use algorithms to solve problems. The problem social media platforms are trying to solve is how to gain and keep your attention. The algorithms take in data based on what you click, what you like, and what you share. They then serve up more content that aligns with your interests to keep you clicking, liking, and sharing away.

In other words, the system is built to please you, not to challenge you.

As a result, we all see more and more and more (and more and endlessly more) news-related content that confirms our worldview and reinforces our ideas (including that the world is a scary or threatened or failing place). It's not only the stories we see. In a perfect world, social media would help us have conversations across economic and racial and social lines. It would allow us to expand our conversations and our horizons. In practice, we build social circles consisting of people who look and think and act like us. We share stories that they like and comment on and share. We, in turn, read stories they share and like, and it's all a vicious cyclone of input that makes us feel that we are right (and popular! And smart! And relevant!). These interactions push all our pleasure triggers, but they are not based on real connections. Meaningful connections with both people and news sources that challenge you lead to deeper self-awareness and growth, not the shallow satisfaction of feeling momentarily validated.

These online echo chambers are dangerous, and they make starting or continuing grace-filled political conversations difficult if not impossible.

We have to exit our echo chambers.

In this chapter we offer accessible challenges to empower people to step outside their own bubbles by engaging with new information sources. We discuss how to talk about politics on Facebook and Twitter in ways that are actually productive. We offer up empathy mapping as a tool for understanding how someone who disagrees with you views the world. We provide suggestions on changing your news sources and interacting with family members, in person and in writing, when you passionately disagree. We discuss the role of politics in our pulpits, workplaces, and church families. This chapter is essential for surviving the holidays and maintaining your friends online and in real life.

It was in the aftermath of the 2016 election that we realized our desires to exit our own echo chambers. Our listeners were also clamoring for ways to push back against a social media environment that left them feeling empty and disconnected. So, only a few weeks after the election, we launched the Exit the Echo Chamber challenge — a weeklong event with our *Pantsuit Politics* community. Every day we posted a different challenge that pushed us outside our own echo chambers on social media, in real life, and in the news media environment.

The daily challenges were:

Day 1 — Take a selfie explaining why you want to exit the echo chamber.

Day 2 — Read three articles from news sources you don't usually read.

Day 3 — Have a conversation in real life with someone who voted differently than you.

Day 4 — Send a letter or email to someone you've disagreed with politically.

Day 5 — Compliment the other side.

Day 6 — Draw an empathy map for someone in another political party.

Day 7 — Take action.

First, we wanted everyone (including ourselves) to think about *why* they wanted to exit the echo chamber by posting a picture of themselves and explaining their reasons for exiting. Much like how the first rules of this book ask you to examine yourself and your motives, we decided the first step of any good challenge is asking yourself why you are doing it in the first place. Sarah posted that she was exiting the echo chamber "because confirmation bias is a threat to our democracy." Beth posted that she was exiting the echo chamber because "narcissism doesn't equal news, and arrogance doesn't equal analysis." We had listeners post that they wanted to exit the echo chamber for reasons that reflected concerns about the media, the political system, and even themselves:

> "Because no political party has a monopoly on good ideas."
> "Because writing off the other half of the population is getting us nowhere."
> "Because I'm guilty of thinking I know it all, and there is so much more to learn."
> "Because I believe empathy is the key to progress."

Next, we encouraged everyone to swap their news sources. We provided a list of podcasts, publications, and writers from both the Left and the Right, and we asked our listeners to swap. Now, this didn't mean we wanted our liberal listeners to engage in a four-hour Rush Limbaugh marathon. We agree with Julia Galef, cofounder of the Center for Applied Rationality, and her recommendation to engage with news sources that aren't directly opposite your worldview and approach — because if you do seek out sources that directly oppose your thinking, you can end up hardening your opinions instead of exploring them. She recommends engaging with news sources through the lens of liberal/ conservative and emotional/analytical. If you are analytical and progressive, try an analytical and conservative news source. If you are conservative and emotional, try a more emotional but also progressive source. For this challenge, we thought it was important to list not the far ideological outreaches of our media environment, but rather sources that are mostly calm and intellectual.

However, even these sources were a challenge at first to many of our listeners. Kyla wrote us about her experience listening to *The Federalist Radio Hour* podcast: "The first [episode] confirmed my worst suspicions of conservatives." It wasn't an immediate revelation. Most of us are decent at articulating the basics of the other side's opinions, even if we lean heavily on emotion and hyperbole. It is only through repeated exposure, helping us to lower our guard and start to really listen, that we can find pieces (even small ones) that we understand and even agree with. That was Kyla's experience with *The Federalist Radio Hour.* She wrote us that she was taking a slow approach to the entire challenge and spent more than a single day on exposing herself to other news sources. She kept listening to *The Federalist Radio Hour* podcast and eventually moved beyond her initial dislike. "The second two were okay, but the one I listened to today actually made some sense and was very timely after having just listened to your podcast and the discussion about how we get our news and what's newsworthy and what's real journalism."[2]

For day three, we asked our listeners to exit the echo chamber by having a real-life conversation with someone they disagree with politically. We kept the mission achievable. The goal was not to score points or convince anyone, but rather to understand why they feel the way they feel.

Here were the tips we offered to our listeners as they tackled this challenge:

- Don't have a stake intellectually, emotionally, or otherwise in the other person's thoughts and feelings. Make "you do you" your mantra.

- When you feel yourself reacting negatively to something you hear, hit pause in your mind. Ask yourself (1) "Why am I reacting this way?" and (2) "What could this conversation be like without my reaction?"
- If you aren't finding common ground, that's fine. Channel your inner talk-show host and conduct a kind, respectful interview of the person. Ask things like: "When did you first start to think about the election that way?" "Have you always voted for this party?" "When you think about future elections, what's really important to you?" "What do you think the biggest challenge for the next four years will be?" "What do you think will be important to shaping the outcome of the midterm elections?"
- Don't make assumptions, and recognize when the other person is making assumptions. When you realize the other person is making a statement based on assumptions about you, call that out: "I understand why you'd think that I support XYZ, since many

people in my party do. But my perspective is different."

- Keep it calm. If you're talking to someone who wants to amp the conversation up, just don't go there. Instead, say things like: "I don't know what you mean when you say [inflammatory term]. Can you share what that means to you?" "Hey, I'm trying to learn from our conversation, not debate. So can you say more about that?" "Do you mind if I take some notes while we talk?" (We don't know why, but trust us! When you start taking notes, it reminds people that having some level of civility is important).

What we found most fascinating from this day of the challenge was that our listeners seemed to fall in two diametrically opposed camps. Either we had listeners who had trouble finding someone they disagreed with politically because they lived in such an echo chamber, *or* they had zero trouble finding someone they disagreed with politically because they were the only person in their family or even community who had voted for their candidate. We wondered afterward if maybe both are a matter of perception more than anything. While we have no doubt that the political silos social scientists have spilled gallons of ink over exist, perhaps they are self-perpetuating in a way. We assume everyone agrees when there are those who may not, but feel intimidated to share their true thoughts. Or we never challenge each other enough to see there are areas of disagreement, something that would surface if we weren't merely patting ourselves on the back about how right we are most of the time.

For day four, we asked our listeners to write a letter to someone they had passionately disagreed with about politics in the past. We wanted people to move beyond the surface-level discussions that happen when someone is a casual acquaintance or Facebook friend. We didn't want people to just recognize where there was honest disagreement around them; we wanted them to dive deep into historical areas of conflict that they had been avoiding in an effort to "keep the peace." This wasn't intended to force people to fight with those they loved most, because this wasn't about fighting. This step was about prioritizing our closest relationships while at the same time prioritizing political debate.

We need to remember — to relearn — what it's like to see the world through the eyes of someone we love even when that is difficult. We need to remember what it is like to disagree with dignity and respect, and we believe that is easiest to do with those we already know and love and trust.

One of our listeners sent an open and vulnerable letter to her mother, whom she had disagreed with over abortion.

Hi Mom,

I've been thinking about this for a few days, and I really appreciate that we were able to talk about the presidential election a little bit the other day. I really appreciated your understanding of my position, even though I'm pretty certain that we voted differently.

There was something I wanted to invite you to reconsider for the future. You mentioned during our conversation that, while you're not a single-issue voter, you had a hard time stomaching Hillary Clinton's position on late-term abortions.

When I watched the third presidential debate, I heard Donald Trump describe a late-term abortion as something horrific that happens with a viable baby days before delivery, and I thought to myself, "That sounds abhorrent and shouldn't happen." And from what I've been able to tell, that does not happen. Viable babies are not aborted days before a woman's due date.

On this issue, I think the majority of people would agree that a woman who changes her mind or gets cold feet thirty weeks into her pregnancy should suck it up, and if she doesn't want her baby, she should put it up for adoption. But, I think that the reality of the situation is a lot closer to what Hillary Clinton described in the debate. Someone who is considering terminating a pregnancy after twenty weeks is facing an impossible choice. These are people who have discovered their baby has a terrible birth defect — maybe their brain isn't developing properly — and they have to decide if they want to carry the baby to term and have their baby die shortly after birth or be kept alive by machine and suffer greatly, or go ahead and let it go and begin the grieving process. Or it's someone who discovers that they have cancer, and they have to decide if they want to begin treatment, which would kill the baby, or delay treatment, which could kill the mother.

I find these realities terrifyingly close

to home. I can put myself in these women's shoes. I have two little girls who need a mother. Would I really be willing to leave Daniel to raise three children by himself? I know that I would jump in front of a moving vehicle, wrestle an alligator, or do whatever it took to protect my children. But in that situation . . . I would want that to be my choice, so that whatever happened, I could put myself and my family in God's hands and go from there. I think that is what the "pro-choice" position is . . . to me, it's a Republican ideal — we have to trust individuals, families, and their doctors to make these heart-wrenching choices together.

I feel like the Republican party has lost its way on this issue by making it so simple: "Protect the life of the baby." We need to support and protect family and women's health. In Texas, the Republican legislature effectively defunded Planned Parenthood, and the maternal mortality rate in Texas jumped 600% because low-income women didn't have access to prenatal health care and screenings. When mothers die having babies, that's bad for babies and families. I also feel like the Republican party has picked another fight in opposing giving women access to birth control under the Affordable Care Act. It just seems like if women who don't want to be pregnant aren't getting pregnant, then they won't get abortions. That seems like a win-win solution!

Anyway, I've been trying to pay attention to both sides of the aisle lately, and there are a lot of Republican and conservative ideas that I would really like to support, but I am perplexed at why the party has chosen Planned Parenthood as a hill to die on. Why do they feel like women will start waiting until the absolute last minute to terminate their pregnancy if only we give them a chance? I'm entirely certain that any woman who feels her baby kick isn't going to end that lightly.

I just wanted to share my thoughts on this with you, because I know you love children, you support families, and you care about people. And I think that our politicians need to know that their constituents are able to handle the complexity of these issues, so they have the freedom to compromise without getting booted out of office. I hope this gives you some food for thought and room for grace on the issue. I love you, and I'm really looking forward to seeing everyone this weekend![3]

When we asked her if and how her mom responded, she reported back that her mother had in fact responded, and she had initially been disappointed that her mother wasn't more responsive and willing to see her side of the issue. "But now that I revisit it, I feel like she gave a little more room than I initially remember (or at least more than is typical for her). I kind of struggled with her response, because who wouldn't secretly hope that such a nice letter might persuade someone not to vote for Donald Trump over the issue of abortion if they had a do-over? But I think that thing you say all the time about 'rubbing each other's rough edges off' really applies here."[4] We were so encouraged by this response, because it's exactly what we've often found in our own exchanges. The first attempt at revisiting difficult topics is harder for us and doesn't always lead to the response we want (okay, it never does initially). That's exactly why they present opportunities for growth. This listener had to face her own fears and be honest about the way she had shut down the conversation in the past without really listening. She had to hear her mother's genuine concerns for babies and consciously prioritize their relationship, not political conversion. When we do this and reflect on our own thoughts and those of others, we will find real opportunities for growth in ourselves and our relationships.

On day five, we asked our listeners to join us in a weekly segment of the show called Compliment the Other Side. One of the central values of our podcast is that both parties serve purposes and contribute important ideas. In order to live out that value, we each take a moment in our Tuesday episodes to compliment a member of the other party. We have complimented senators speaking their minds, governors solving big problems, state representatives and local officials working hard on everything from school lunches to tax reform. When we asked our listeners to take part, they seemed to have lists on hand and were ready and willing to look beyond the national names getting all the attention (and perpetuating our polarization) to people in their own communities and states doing inspiring work. Complimenting the other side is one of the most refreshing parts of our podcast, and it became a favorite moment in this challenge.

On day six, we took a different approach to our exploration. We often talk about having increased empathy for the other side, and we felt that exiting the echo chamber only to hear ideas and emotions you could not understand would not be a positive step forward. Sarah first came across the idea of empathy maps while listening to a sales podcast. Dave Gray, a management consultant and author, originally created empathy maps as a tool to help sales teams understand their customers. Sarah was also reading *Strangers in Their Own Land: Anger and Mourning on the American Right.* The book is author and sociologist Arlie Russell Hochschild's effort to exit the echo chamber by moving to rural Louisiana. Sarah started thinking about what Hochschild described as "empathy walls" and how to climb them in our political discussions. Empathy maps seemed like a good approach.

An empathy map is a tool used to gain deeper insight into a point of view. Empathy means that you can both intellectually understand someone else's feelings and vicariously experience those feelings. We asked our listeners to identify one political opinion or group that they struggled to understand and to use the empathy map to gain insight into that point of view. Creating

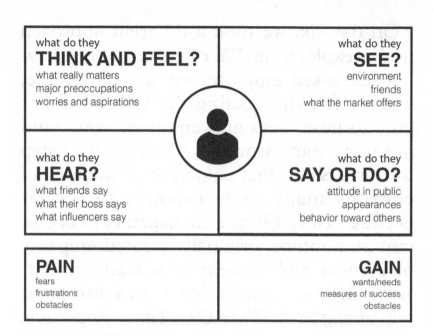

what do they **THINK AND FEEL?**	what do they **SEE?**
what really matters major preoccupations worries and aspirations	environment friends what the market offers
what do they **HEAR?**	what do they **SAY OR DO?**
what friends say what their boss says what influencers say	attitude in public appearances behavior toward others

PAIN	**GAIN**
fears frustrations obstacles	wants/needs measures of success obstacles

an empathy map allows you to tune in to another person by considering what that person thinks, sees, hears, and feels. You also consider the person's "pains and gains."

Many of our listeners told us that actually putting pen to paper and thinking through the perspective of the other side forced them to push themselves past the usual emotions of the argument. Many looked at editorials and reached out to friends and family to really flesh out the areas with which they struggled to empathize. Like every other day's challenge, the empathy map wasn't a cure-all. None of these challenges are a magic pill in and of themselves. Instead, they help bit by bit to lay the foundation for better understanding of both ourselves and others.

On the final day of the challenge, we asked our listeners to take action. The best way to exit the echo chamber of opinions is to exit in the purest sense of the word. Stop talking and start doing. While we believe whole-heartedly in the power of dialogue, there is a time when closing your computer or putting down your phone and stepping out into the real world is the best way to exit the echo chamber. Action can take many forms, and we encouraged our community to find the action best suited to their time and energy. We had listeners call their congressional representatives for the first time. We had people attend local city council and school board meetings. We had people sign up for elected-official training programs. Whatever action they took, the willingness to stop politically existing solely inside an echo chamber was key to exiting for good.

YOUR PRACTICE

Take the Exit the Echo Chamber challenge yourself! Our listener Kyla suggested a *slow version:* "I felt I needed to put a lot more planning and thought into each step than I could manage in a day (or two!)." We love that, so feel free to dedicate as much time as you need to each step. Be easy on yourself and others. We exist inside an intense media environment, reinforced on so many levels by the ways in which we sort ourselves socially in real life and online. Take your time and give yourself lots of grace in the process. Here is a list of suggestions to get you started on your own exit:

- We still love to hear from people exiting the echo chamber. So take a selfie explaining why you want to exit the echo chamber, include the hashtag #exittheechochamber, and tag us on your favorite social media platform.
- Read three articles from news sources you don't usually read.
- Have a conversation in real life with someone who voted differently than you.
- Send a letter or email to someone you've disagreed with politically.
- Compliment the other side. This is another great social media post and encourages a completely different energy than you usually find surrounding politics in this medium.
- Draw an empathy map for someone in another political party.
- Take action.

CONTINUE THE CONVERSATION

From a spiritual perspective, we are specifically called to exit our echo chambers. Think about the life and practices of Jesus. He shared messages that completely shook many religious leaders' understanding of faith. He wrecked the temple to point out its misuse. And he specifically reached out to people otherwise shunned by society. We love telling our children the story of Zacchaeus specifically because it's an exit the echo chamber moment. There are myriad reasons to reach beyond the people and sources that make us comfortable so that we can test and refine and enhance our own understandings.

1. An echo chamber can be defined in many different ways — all of which have their own political repercussions. How often do you engage with someone of a different race or economic status? If you are married with kids, how often do you talk with single people or those who have chosen to be childless?
2. What are your fears (if you have any) about engaging with someone outside your political perspective?
3. How do your usual news sources make you feel? Before you turn on the TV or

click through to the site, do you feel anxiety or geared up in some way, or can you approach it with a more neutral emotional position?

CHAPTER TEN:
KEEP IT NUANCED

When we started *Pantsuit Politics,* we thought of *nuance* as a noun. *Nuance* meant finding the subtleties in arguments, being open to shades of gray, and moving past political talking points. As we have grown our community and our understanding of each other, we've realized that we need to treat *nuance* as a verb. It is a lifelong practice. Like exercising or playing the piano, engaging in nuanced discussions requires constant conditioning and attention to the fundamentals.

The principles we've set forth in this book provide the foundation for your practice. You're equipped to examine what informs your political views and to develop those views based on your values, rather than defaulting to a party affiliation. You're ready to treat yourself and others with grace and to participate meaningfully in political conversation and work while keeping it in perspective. You're prepared to hear and respectfully consider opinions that challenge you from a variety of sources. You value expertise, and you value your own perspective and experiences.

Now you have to do it. Over and over again, you'll need to repeat this cycle. Working your way through this process will develop intellectual, emotional, and spiritual muscles. Sometimes you'll overdo it and need a break. Sometimes your muscles will feel stronger and more flexible than others. We experience these changes and challenges in ourselves. Even on a consistent schedule of talking to each other about difficult subjects, we have off days. We annoy ourselves and each other on certain topics, and pushing back against our instincts to be representatives of our parties is a constant struggle.

We are always pushing ourselves. Our listeners sometimes think we push too far past our party boundaries. When we discussed rape on college campuses and asked whether the emphasis on punitive measures actually helps rape culture, some of our listeners were outraged. We have tried to consider not only the gravity of the threat a nuclear North Korea poses to the United States, but also why North Korea might feel threatened by the United States. We have tried to put ourselves in the shoes of NFL athletes protesting police brutality during the national anthem and in the shoes of families of officers who have been killed while protecting their communities. We have tried to see the world from the perspective of students in Syria and Iran, because the world is not a stage for American drama.

The practice of nuance means asking painful, difficult questions — questions that might reveal something new or bring a position into different relief or otherwise illuminate our perspectives. We don't always or even often advocate for policies that align with our conclusions, and often we don't reach conclusions. We ask questions simply because we think too few questions are being asked in America. We don't want to participate in a race to sell answers. The process of asking these questions will necessarily involve mistakes and discomfort. It is a stripping away of our programming so that we can inhabit our souls while we grapple with the experiment of living together in a democratic society.

Talking about politics is hard because we're humans talking to other humans. We're a mess — a glorious mess of emotions and life experiences and family histories and stresses and habits and beliefs. The more we practice nuanced conversation, the more we realize that the whole mess needs to be at and on the table. We are at our worst when we pretend to be neutral or unemotional about a topic. Our discussions are more effective when we are radically transparent about the aspects of our personalities and lives that color our perspectives. Sarah likes to say there is literally nothing she won't talk about, and she's brought Beth along with her. *Pantsuit Politics* listeners know all about the car accident Beth experienced at age seventeen and about the shooting at Sarah's high school, because these tragedies are integral parts of who we are and how we view the world. They also know about our faith. We return throughout our conversations and in this book to what faith means to us, because it is inextricably linked to our values and policy ideals.

We've had a very hard time talking about our faith on the podcast — we never want anyone to feel excluded or put off by those discussions. There is a distinct frustration in America with expressions like "thoughts and prayers." We understand that frustration. We are also not interested in leaving or able to leave our faith behind. We've learned that most people warmly embrace honesty.

We share where we are. We share that we don't expect everyone to agree with us. We try to share as explicitly as possible what faith means to us. During Hurricane Harvey, we saw several people saying versions of, "What does one pray for regarding a hurricane?" Rather than being up in arms about questions like this one, we try to explain how we pray. We explain that we almost never pray "for" anything but we pray because it connects us to a loving presence that is greater than we are. We pray because it is the best way we know to send love into the world. When we drop our defensiveness about prayer, we find that people who vehemently disagree with our beliefs still respect them.

We also try to take care in our language. When president Donald Trump was inaugurated, he spoke about "American carnage," referring to the economic losses our country experienced as a result of a decline in manufacturing. Months later, bullets rained down from a hotel room in Las Vegas onto a crowd attending a country music concert. The Las Vegas shooter killed 58 people and injured 489 people. This was actual American carnage. It matters when we use words like *evil, enemy,* and *ally.* When we talk about terrorism, what do we really mean?

Do we mean the involvement of a foreign power, or violence motivated by politics? In an era filled with hyperbole, media noise, and brutal assumptions about the people around us, being precise in our language is a revolutionary act. It is revolutionary to use words calibrated to the circumstances, because doing so keeps us grounded. To put it in language Beth uses with her children, we can be at a two instead of a nine.

We do the best we can, and we repeat the practices of giving ourselves grace and being comfortable with our discomfort. When we're wrong, we admit it and move on. When we lose our nuance, we acknowledge it. We keep going, expecting setbacks and using those setbacks to make us better thinkers, speakers, people, and friends.

We've realized that embracing the mess and mixing the emotional and spiritual with the political is distinctly feminine. When we tried to introduce male guests on the podcast on a more regular basis, we heard from listeners — particularly from male listeners — that they didn't enjoy the conversation as much. Male listeners shared with us that they have never had an opportunity to hear two women talk this openly, uninterrupted and uninfluenced by men, and they saw the value in this new approach. An iTunes reviewer once referred to us as "godmothers of a new genre."[1] We hope that review was prescient, because the kind of conversations we're encouraging you to have in this book will get America's political car out of the ditch and back on the road. Conflict sells, but conciliation creates progress.

The kind of practice we're discussing is not a magic potion that will solve every problem in our country. It is a practice that will open up opportunities for problem-solving. We believe that America has all the brain power needed to address environmental changes, harness the power of technology while mitigating its downsides, and adapt to economic evolution. We also know that America has thought leaders, teachers, pastors, ethicists, and artists to help us deal with discrimination and oppression. We need to open the doors for those conversations, and we need you to walk through those doors with all your skills, ideas, and experiences. We have to stop fearing difficult discussions and start seeing them as opportunities for growth.

Saturday Night Live captured America's tortured relationship with tough subjects in a sketch about the #MeToo movement.[2] In the sketch, three couples were enjoying dinner together until one member of the party brought up an article about Aziz Ansari's sexual encounter with a young woman referred to as Grace. The encounter was described by babe.net in excruciating detail[3] and instantly became a lightning rod. Some individuals viewed Ansari's conduct as predatory.[4] Others saw the babe.net piece as a disappointed lover unfairly slamming Ansari for not being into her.[5] In the sketch, the mention of Ansari's name sent chills through the previously jovial diners. Each person tried to express thoughts, only to be warned, *"Careful!"* by their companions. SNL perfectly portrayed the awkwardness and fear that accompanies conversations about sex, consent, and power in sexual relationships.

We discussed the Ansari story on the podcast and received record-setting feedback. So many women and men wrote to us, some to litigate the facts of the encounter, some to share their own hurtful and confusing experiences, and many to ask whether and how the disconnect in perspectives between men and women can be bridged. Initially the #MeToo movement had been about holding powerful men accountable who had clearly abused their power through often criminal actions over a number of years and with numerous victims. The standard for accountability shifted with new revelations, and the Ansari story felt to many men and women like the court of public opinion had gone too far.

If America is to genuinely reckon with the imbalance of power between men and women that often leads to sexual abuse, we need to be able to talk about the Ansari story over dinners everywhere. We don't need to do this in salacious or personal ways. Our interest is not in shaming Ansari or Grace, or even thinking about Ansari and Grace. This story struck so many nerves because it is so relatable, so morally ambiguous, so fraught with questions about the decisions two people made in a private moment. Leave Ansari and Grace out of the story. Leave sex out of the story. An encounter in which a man is pressuring a woman to act in a certain way, and the woman is conflicted about how to respond, and the man doesn't think he is pressuring the woman, and the woman experiences the pressure as intense and possibly threatening is the story of gender relations. We can all do better in our interactions with one another, and some of us can do better than others.

We don't need to decide who was right

and wrong, or who was more wrong, or whether Ansari's career should be impacted, or whether Grace should have talked to that reporter. So many journalists and pundits have opined that the babe.net piece hurt the #MeToo movement. We can understand that mind-set: "Win the war, not the battle." "This one isn't the hill to die on." "This fight isn't worth our capital." Those phrases all conjure a mentality of violence, fear, and scarcity. They hold us back from better understanding each other.

Whether we are talking about gender, race, sexuality, or other ways in which some of us hold more or less power than others by virtue of identity, defensiveness arises. When we are told that we have power by virtue of our identity, we recoil. It feels accusatory: "You've done something wrong just by being you." We also recoil from hearing that we have less power by virtue of our identity because it feels condescending: "You're going to have a hard time just because you're you." That personal defensiveness is reinforced in cultural commentary. Stories about sexual abuse have borne this out. Reactions include "men can't even say hello without being labeled predators," "women are being treated like infants who can't take care of themselves," "people are being fired without due process, and now anyone can make an accusation that ruins someone else's life," and "who paid her to smear him?"

This heightened defensive mode produces the kind of awkwardness mirrored in the SNL sketch. We all have stories where we said or did the wrong thing and someone got hurt. When the headlines remind us of our "complicity," we struggle and often shut down. We both try to drop the impulse to either shut down or overly shame ourselves. It helps us to remember we are all doing the best we can, and every situation is a complex mix of individual choices and societal influences.

We want to teach our children to handle adversity and their own mistakes with a combination of responsibility, grace, and resolve. If you read the Aziz Ansari story and see yourself in the Ansari role, it's okay to say (as Ansari essentially has), "I did not understand that I was hurting another person at the time. I see now that I did. I will learn from this so that I don't hurt someone else again."[6] You are not a bad person because you made a mistake. You are a growing, evolving, loving person when you're able to fully accept mistakes and learn from them.

Just as growing from our mistakes requires acknowledgement of those mistakes, learning how our behaviors impact other people so that we don't repeat mistakes requires listening. We don't lose anything when we listen. If you are a man, acknowledging that women have perspectives based on experiences they've had and you haven't does not in any way diminish you. Hearing that you have unconsciously or unintentionally said things that made women uncomfortable does not condemn you. If we can all come to the table understanding that we do not and are not expected to know everything, we can learn from one another. The two of us can each acknowledge that we are white women from middle-class backgrounds living in Kentucky, worshipping in Christian churches with our children and our husbands, and that those factors both inform and limit our perspectives. We don't have to apologize for any of those limitations to be aware of them and to be interested in expanding our understandings of people with different perspectives.

Practicing nuance to have transformative conversations about sex requires us to work with every principle we've described. First, we have to be willing to have the conversations. It has been shocking and sad to learn that many victims of predatory sexual behavior have spent decades dealing with their abuse alone. It also perpetuates the problem. How many rapes, assaults, and abuses could have been stopped if we encouraged and supported people who share what happened to them?

We have to take our jerseys off. We can't possibly think that abuse is a partisan issue; it is a human issue. We also need to let go of the idea that #MeToo is only a women's issue or conversation. Taking off our traditionally gendered jerseys is important. When we put on our jerseys about #MeToo conversations, we're choosing to disconnect from our own experiences and the experiences of the people around us in favor of mimicking media personalities. We need to show up in these discussions as ourselves.

We must fully flesh out our values to understand why we are discussing these issues. Why does encouraging people who have been abused by others to talk about that abuse matter? Don't we all share a desire for all people to be treated with dignity, to have others respect their bodies and spirits? You might share those values and feel that the Ansari story was too much — that's okay. Finding your why isn't dictating an outcome; it's establishing a foundation for a shared connection in processing information and working toward solutions.

Keeping politics in its place is a key to grappling with sexual power and abuse. That looks different for each of us. During the height of the #MeToo conversation, Sarah felt emotional catharsis in seeing individual perpetrators held accountable. Beth was reluctant to dive into the details of any given situation, feeling a sense of sadness and empathy for the individuals involved (as both victims and perpetrators) and their families. We both had to take breaks from the coverage and surround ourselves with other activities and interests to avoid being overly immersed in it in ways that were not healthy.

Grace helps us hold the tension in conversations about sex. We can prioritize healing and forgiveness while demanding accountability and acceptance of responsibility. When punishment is called for (as it sometimes is), we can impose that punishment justly, and we can acknowledge that people should not be solely defined by their worst instincts and actions. We can look at our own behaviors, question ourselves, and still love ourselves. For people of faith, we can remember that this is how God sees us — flawed, sometimes reckless, always beloved.

We've also developed some specific ideas about curiosity in connection with #MeToo conversations. We think that it is important and frustratingly difficult to hear each other out because sex is so personal. The following five commitments can open and enhance discussions:

1. Commit to recognizing and putting down your defensiveness.
2. Commit to learning something in the discussion.
3. Commit to having a dialogue instead of giving alternate speeches.
4. Commit to assessing whether you're the right person to say what is on your mind. (Sometimes the answer is no.)
5. Commit to ending the discussion knowing that you have strengthened the relationship.

We think these commitments can foster meaningful dialogue in the context of any relationship if participants in the discussion genuinely embrace them.

The conversations will be filled with paradox. It can be true that a person in a sexual encounter both likes and, on some level, fears their potential partner. It is true that sexual relationships in the workplace are generally a bad idea, and it's also true that many people fall in love with coworkers and develop long-lasting, mutually rewarding, loving relationships. It can be true that two people had consensual sex, and that one person abused their power in participating in that sex. It is true that some behavior is not criminal but still violative. It is true that sex can lead to countless problems in our lives and that it is one of the most beautiful things two people can share. The pool of discussing sex has a huge deep end, and we have to be willing to swim in it.

One reason we have so many problems with and because of sex is that we avoid discussing it. Talking about sex is inherently uncomfortable. We receive messages that sex is dirty, taboo. We also receive messages that keeping sex "a little bit bad" is critical to it being pleasurable. We learn that men take sex and women give it, and that men taking is natural while women giving is shameful. It is a significant stretch for all of us to have healthy conversations about sex, especially since many of us can't fully articulate our own feelings about it. We can be honest about that and do the best we can, knowing that over time these discussions will become more precise and productive.

When we do talk about sex, we're almost always doing it in echo chambers. Those echo chambers — the community of a few close friends or the clichéd locker room — become even more closed and unhealthy because the topic is so personal and uncomfortable. So the conversations that we do have about sex tend to reinforce the way that sex is portrayed in media. We become more entrenched in existing ideas and drift further from our actual experiences. Leaving these echo chambers is essential to moving the conversation forward. That might mean talking to your mom, your pastor, your therapist. It means that men and women have to communicate with each other in platonic relationships about good sex and bad sex, consent, and desire. It means that workplaces have to do more than compliance training on sexual harassment. They have to set and enforce standards of conduct that create a culture in which people know their boundaries and feel supported and welcomed to call out people crossing those boundaries.

Working our way through this process, we can handle discussing different kinds of conduct without needing to litigate and sanction all of that conduct. We're able to separate out the process that would apply in a civil or criminal proceeding from the standards that we want to uphold in our businesses, organizations, and governments. It leads to us being able to understand how all our interactions with one another influence respect, power, and agency. When we get to that level of conversation, we can consciously create and model partnerships that are filled with integrity and equality.

We have the power to transform how men and women relate to each other in order to dramatically reduce gender-based violence. And the lesson for us is that we have the power to transform almost every aspect of our culture that doesn't work today. School shootings are not inevitable. Partisan gridlock is not predestined. Mistrust in our government and other institutions is not part of the natural law. We can fix these things. Working together, we can build a future that makes us proud and establishes a solid foundation for future generations.

We've decided to stop calling America "divided." Buying into this conflict-driven narrative is a choice, and it's a choice we're not going to make. We don't feel divided from each other or the people in our lives in any way. There are no perfect relationships, ideas, people, or organizations in our lives. They're all flawed, just as we are flawed. But we see past those flaws — because we are first looking for the good. We don't size up our husbands, friends, family members, or neighbors based on their stances on nuclear proliferation.

Yes, there are differences in America — even in our values. We are better for those differences. Our system needs a party that embraces federal policy to solve problems and a party that works to restrain federal power. We need people who champion the private sector and people who advocate for more public works. The US Constitution is premised on balance. We need everyone.

There are some deal-breakers and bright lines. As we discussed in chapter 8, no one's inherent dignity should be threatened or violated. In the landscape of policy issues, these are exceptions rather than the rule. When we pretend otherwise, we acquiesce to a house divided against itself. We need a radical embrace of our shared humanity to move us out of the battle and into community.

We hope that you'll take up this call to action earnestly. Together, we can invigorate our interests in virtue and spread grace-filled conversation throughout our city halls, the halls of Congress, and even those Thanksgiving dinners. In the process, we will find each other and ourselves. It will not be easy, and it will require growth. We will evolve individually and collectively, and we'll get closer to that more perfect union our founding fathers and mothers envisioned — one that is united without being unanimous. That is the promise of nuance. That is the power of saying, "I think you're wrong, but I'm listening."

CONTINUE THE CONVERSATION

We hope that you feel ready to use the tools in this book to develop nuanced conversations about politics in your lives. We hope you feel inspired. We need you to bring all your thoughts and energy to developing a greater sense of community in our country.

Review the rules outlined in this book, and think of them as a process on repeat:

- We Should Talk About Politics
- Take Off Your Jersey
- Find Your Why
- Put Politics in Its Place
- Give Grace
- Get Curious
- Embrace the Paradox

- Get Comfortable with Being Uncomfortable
- Exit the Echo Chamber
- Keep It Nuanced

Identify three action steps you plan to take to incorporate these rules into your political engagement.

Thank you again for trusting us to discuss politics with you. We hope you'll stay at our virtual kitchen table with us. Until we talk with you again, keep it nuanced, y'all.

ACKNOWLEDGMENTS

SARAH'S ACKNOWLEDGMENTS

It's not easy being a little girl who likes to talk politics. Thank you to everyone who listened and encouraged me to keep talking. I have particularly vivid memories of long conversations about JFK, FDR, and the working man with my grandfather Ollie Stewart. Thank you, Papa. Thank you to my parents — all three of them — for answering my questions and debating with me far past the requirements of good parenting. Thank you to my grandmothers Betty and Nancy for loving me wholly and completely without condition. Thank you to every teacher who taught me to think, to speak, and to write, especially Stacey Marshall, Toby Dulworth, and Kim Miller.

My childhood was shaped by many people who took the time to listen to and encourage me, but my adulthood has been shaped largely by one. Thank you to my husband

Nicholas Holland, who has the sharpest mind and kindest heart of any person I know. Right after "Will you marry me?" "Why don't you start a podcast?" has to be the best question I've ever been asked, and both questions were asked by him. Thank you, Nicholas, for supporting me, encouraging me, and loving me. I adore you.

Thank you to my sons Griffin, Amos, and Felix for raising the stakes on everything I do. Work only matters if I'm making the world a better place for you.

Thank you to my beloved sister friends — Elizabeth, Annie, and Laura — when things go bad, you are who I call. Thanks for always answering.

Thank you to the community of Paducah, Kentucky. My village. My tribe. My heart. Thank you for giving me the most magnificent place to practice the lessons of this book.

Thank you to our listeners for giving me grace over years of *ummms,* "likes", and plain old screwups. You make me better. Thank you to Sharon — we simply wouldn't be here without you. Thank you to Jessica and the team at Thomas Nelson for seeing our vision and believing in it.

Thank you to Beth. Thank you for saying yes to every new adventure. Thank you for listening. Thank you for being patient and wise and brave.

BETH'S ACKNOWLEDGMENTS

When I was young and not exactly engaged by a sermon in church, my mom would grab a bulletin and jot down a writing prompt. Because of her prompts, I wrote hundreds of essays on offering envelopes and around the margins of prayer lists. Mom read every word and offered critiques, teaching me to be more persuasive, more succinct, and clearer. She did the same thing with each chapter of this book. Thank you, Sharon Thurman. You taught me how to be a writer, and you taught me that what I have to say matters.

Thank you to Kimberly Rocks and Kelly Thurman, who have been cheering me on throughout this process. When you two say you are proud of me, I know I'm succeeding by life's most important metrics.

Thank you to Dr. Susan Ward Diamond for renewing my faith in the church and bringing nuance to my understanding of Scripture. Thank you to Tracey Puthoff, James Zimmerman, and Caitlin Felvus for your wise counsel and belief in me throughout this process. Thank you to Kelly McCallum for treating our children like they

299

are your own so that I'm able to do the work I love. Thank you to Alise Napp for your insightful and enthusiastic review.

Sharon Pelletier has been more than an agent. She loved this book into being before the first sentence was written. Thank you, Sharon, for making this possible. Jessica Wong, Brigitta Nortker, and Karin Silver improved our writing every time they touched it. Thank you for your care and consideration at every step.

My understanding of grace and love has been infinitely expanded by the way my husband, Chad, has handled my dream of changing political conversation. Thank you for your sacrifices and support and patience and humor. Thank you to my curious, witty, exuberant daughters, Jane and Ellen, for understanding all the quiet that I request and for being the best teachers I've ever had.

Finally, thank you, Sarah. I adore and trust you and hope that we are only beginning to learn and create together.

NOTES

Chapter 1: We Should Talk Politics

1. Hannah Arendt, *On Revolution* (1963; New York: Penguin Books, 1990), 119. Emphasis added.
2. "Abigail Adams to John Adams, 14 August 1776," Adams Papers, National Archives, accessed June 18, 2018, https://founders.archives.gov/documents/Adams/04-02-02-0058.
3. "A League of Their Own Quotes," IMDb, accessed June 18, 2018, https://www.imdb.com/title/tt0104694/quotes.
4. "#Nuance," August 7, 2015, http://sarahstewartholland.com/blog/nuance.
5. "Dear Mattie Show 85: Sarah & Beth from Pantsuit Politics and How to Keep Calm in Political Engaging," *The Dear Mattie Show,* February 1, 2017, http://www.dearmattieshow.com/podcasts/dear-mattie-show-85-sarah-beth-pantsuit

-politics-and-how-keep-calm-political
-engaging/.
6. "Abigail Adams to John Quincy Adams, 19 January 1780," Adams Papers, National Archives, accessed June 19, 2018, https://founders.archives.gov/documents/Adams/04–03–02–0207.

Chapter 2: Take Off Your Jersey

1. Bob Bryan and Joe Perticone, "A Top Senate Republican Just Threw Cold Water on the Hail Mary Plan to Avoid a Shutdown," *Business Insider Singapore,* January 19, 2018, https://www.businessinsider.sg/ government-shutdown-2018-cornyn-says-no-to-back-up-plan-short-term-bill-2018-1/.
2. Mark Landler and Rick Gladstone, "Chemicals Would Be 'Game Changer' in Syria, Obama Says," *New York Times,* March 20, 2013, https://www.nytimes.com/2013/03/21/world/middleeast/syria-developments.html.
3. Paul McLeary, "The Slam Dunk Contest," *Guardian,* April 27, 2007, https://www.theguardian.com/commentisfree/2007/apr/27/theslamdunkcontest1.
4. Steven Rogers, "National Forces in State Legislative Elections," *ANNALS of the*

American Academy of Political and Social Science 667, no. 1 (August 2016): 207–25, https://doi.org/10.1177/00027162 16662454.

5. "The Partisan Divide on Political Values Grows Even Wider," Pew Research Center, October 5, 2017, http://www.people -press.org/2017/10/05/the-partisan-divide -on-political-values-grows-even-wider.

6. Stephen G. Bloom, "Lesson of a Lifetime," *Smithsonian,* September 2005, https://www.smithsonianmag.com/science -nature/lesson-of-a-lifetime-72754306/.

7. Quoted in Charles M. Blow, " 'Politics Is a Team Sport,' " *Campaign Stops* (blog), *New York Times,* February 23, 2012, https://campaignstops.blogs.nytimes.com/ 2012/02/23/politics-is-a-team-sport/.

8. Clio Andris et al., "The Rise of Partisanship and Super-Cooperators in the U.S. House of Representatives," *PLoS ONE* 10, no. 4 (April 2015): 5, https://doi.org/10 .1371/journal.pone.0123507.

9. Tim Alberta, "John Boehner Unchained," *Politico Magazine,* November/December 2017, https://www.politico.com/magazine/ story/2017/10/29/john-boehner-trump -house-republican-party-retirement -profile-feature-215741.

10. Charles Franklin Benvegar, in Vincent

Godfrey Burns, comp., *The Songs of the Free State Bards* (Washington: New World Books, 1967).

11. Franklin D. Roosevelt, "Annual Message to Congress," January 4, 1935, The American Presidency Project, http://www.presidency.ucsb.edu/ws/?pid=14890.

12. Dylan Matthews, " 'If the Goal Was to Get Rid of Poverty, We Failed': The Legacy of the 1996 Welfare Reform," Vox, June 20, 2016, https://www.vox.com/2016/6/20/11789988/clintons-welfare-reform.

13. Arthur C. Brooks, "The Dignity Deficit: Reclaiming Americans' Sense of Purpose," *Foreign Affairs,* March/April 2017, https://www.foreignaffairs.com/articles/united-states/2017–02–13/dignity-deficit.

14. Barb Darrow, "The Bright Side of Job-Killing Automation," *Fortune,* April 5, 2017, http://fortune.com/2017/04/05/jobs-automation-artificial-intelligence-robotics/.

15. National Federation of Independent Business, cited in Rob Kaplan, "America Has to Close the Workforce Skills Gap," *Bloomberg,* April 12, 2017, https://www.bloomberg.com/view/articles/2017-04-12/america-has-to-close-the-workforce-skills-gap.

16. Audrey Watters, "The Invented History

of 'The Factory Model of Education,' "
Hack Education, April 25, 2015, http://
hackeducation.com/2015/04/25/factory
-model.

17. Drive to 55 Alliance, accessed May 17,
2018, http://driveto55.org/.

18. We recommend listening to "The Frack-
ing Boom, a Baby Boom, and the Retreat
from Marriage" on *Freakonomics Radio*
with Melissa Kearney, professor of economics at the University of Maryland, for
a modern and important take on this
topic, http://www.freakonomics.com/
podcast/fracking-baby-boom-retreat
-marriage/.

19. "Prioritizing Grace," *Pantsuit Politics,*
August 25, 2016, http://www.pantsuit
politicsshow.com/new-blog/2016/8/25/
prioritizing-grace.

20. Michelle Chen, "Could a Universal
Basic Income Work in the US?," *Nation,*
August 15, 2017, https://www.thenation
.com/article/could-a-universal-basic
-income-work-in-the-us/.

21. Richard Rohr, "From Disconnection to
Connection," September 15, 2016, Center
for Action and Contemplation, https://cac
.org/from-disconnection-to-connection
-2016-09-15/.

22. "Fire and Fury, Oprah for President,

and Faith and Politics with Michael Wear,"
Pantsuit Politics, January 9, 2018, http://
www.pantsuitpoliticsshow.com/show
-archives/2018/1/9/fire-and-fury-oprah-for
-president-and-faith-and-politics-with
-michael-wear.
23. Mark 14:8 AMP.

Chapter 3: Find Your Why

1. Paul E. Peterson et al., "Ten-Year Trends in Public Opinion from the EdNext Poll," *Education Next* 17, no. 1 (Winter 2017), http://educationnext.org/ten-year-trends -in-public-opinion-from-ednext-poll-2016 -survey/.
2. Peterson et al.
3. Andrew Tyndall, "Issues? What Issues?" *Tyndall Report* (blog), October 25, 2016, http://tyndallreport.com/comment/20/ 5778/.
4. Thomas E. Patterson, "News Coverage of the 2016 General Election: How the Press Failed the Voters," Shorenstein Center, December 7, 2016, https://shorenstein center.org/news-coverage-2016-general -election/.
5. Jeff Stein, "Study: Hillary Clinton's TV Ads Were Almost Entirely Policy-Free," Vox, March 8, 2017, https://www.vox.com/

policy-and-politics/2017/3/8/14848636/
hillary-clinton-tv-ads.

6. Wikipedia, s.v. "Harry and Louise," last modified November 6, 2017, 19:35, https://en.wikipedia.org/wiki/Harry_and _Louise.

7. "Harry and Louise on Clinton's Health Plan," YouTube video, 1:00, posted by danieljbmitchell, July 15, 2007, https:// www.youtube.com/watch?v=Dt31nhle eCg.

8. Martha Shanahan, "5 Memorable Moments When Town Hall Meetings Turned to Rage," NPR, August 7, 2013, https:// www.npr.org/sections/itsallpolitics/2013/ 08/07/209919206/5-memorable-moments -when-town-hall-meetings-turned-to-rage.

9. Text of Facebook post available at Dan Farber, "Palin Weighs In on Health Care Reform," CBS News, August 8, 2009, https://www.cbsnews.com/news/palin -weighs-in-on-health-care-reform/.

10. Angie Drobnic Holan, "PolitiFact's Lie of the Year: 'Death Panels'," PolitiFact, December 18, 2009, http://www.politifact .com/truth-o-meter/article/2009/dec/18/ politifact-lie-year-death-panels/.

11. Atul Gawande, "Overkill," *New Yorker,* May 11, 2015, https://www.newyorker .com/magazine/2015/05/11/overkill-atul

-gawande.

12. Bradley Sawyer and Cynthia Cox, "How Does Health Spending in the U.S. Compare to Other Countries?" Peterson-Kaiser Health System Tracker, February 13, 2018, https://www.healthsystemtracker .org/chart-collection/health-spending-u-s -compare-countries.

13. To be fair, it's not all bad news. The US performs better than other countries on a number of metrics, including several statistics relative to cancer survival. See Sawyer and Gonzales, "How Does the Quality of the U.S. Healthcare System Compare to Other Countries?"

14. "American's #1 Health Problem," American Institute of Stress, accessed May 10, 2018, https://www.stress.org/ americas-1-health-problem/.

15. "Stop Protecting the Employer-Based Healthcare System," *Washington Examiner,* March 9, 2017, https://www.washington examiner.com/stop-protecting-the-em ployer-based-healthcare-system.

16. Simon Sinek, "Start with Why: How Great Leaders Inspire Everyone to Take Action," filmed at TEDxPuget Sound, September 2009, video, 17:58, https:// www.ted.com/talks/simon_sinek_how _great_leaders_inspire_action.

Chapter 4: Put Politics in Its Place

1. Paul E. Peterson et al., "Ten-Year Trends in Public Opinion from the EdNext Poll," *Education Next* 17, no. 1 (Winter 2017), http://educationnext.org/ten-year-trends -in-public-opinion-from-ednext-poll-2016 -survey/.
2. "Religion," Gallup, accessed June 20, 2018, http://news.gallup.com/poll/1690/ religion.aspx.
3. Art Swift, "Americans' Trust in Mass Media Sinks to New Low," Gallup, September 14, 2016, http://news.gallup.com/ poll/195542/americans-trust-mass-media -sinks-new-low.aspx.
4. J. D. Vance, *Hillbilly Elegy* (New York: HarperCollins, 2016), 194.
5. Vance, 142.
6. David A. Graham, "Why Ordinary Citizens Are Acting as First Responders in Houston," *Atlantic,* August 28, 2017, https://www.theatlantic.com/politics/ archive/2017/08/ordinary-citizens-are-first -responders/538233/.
7. Graham.
8. Amanda Young, "Prison Choir Captures Gold in World Choir Games," WLWT5 News, July 13, 2012, http://www.wlwt .com/article/prison-choir-captures-gold-in

-world-choir-games/3523719.
9. "There Will Be a Wednesday," *Pantsuit Politics,* November 6, 2016, http://www .pantsuitpoliticsshow.com/new-blog/2016/ 11/6/there-will-be-a-wednesday.

Chapter 5: Give Grace

1. "Buechner Themes: Hope Through Grace," Frederick Buechner (website), accessed May 11, 2018, http://www .frederickbuechner.com/hope-through -grace/. Originally published in Buechner's book *Wishful Thinking* (New York: Harper & Row, 1973).
2. Michael Wear, "Pro-Life Voters and Pro-Choice Politicians," *Michael Wear* (blog), December 14, 2017, http://michaelwear .com/blog/2017/12/14/pro-life-voters-and -pro-choice-politicians.
3. "Special Guest Bob Inglis on Climate Change and Free Enterprise," *Pantsuit Politics,* October 7, 2016, http://www .pantsuitpoliticsshow.com/show-archives/ 2016/10/7/season-2-episode-20-special -guest-bob-inglis-on-climate-change-and -free-enterprise?rq=bob%20.
4. "Brother David Steindl-Rast: Happiness Begins with Gratitude," *Oprah's SuperSoul Conversations* (podcast), October 30,

2017, https://www.youtube.com/watch ?v=4YxT-mZi1bU.

5. "A Response to Christopher, Who Says We Are Fake News," *Pantsuit Politics,* April 27, 2017, http://www.pantsuitpolitics show.com/new-blog/2017/4/27/a-response -to-christopher-who-says-we-are-fake -news.

6. "The Great Redhead Debate," *Pantsuit Politics,* September 19, 2016, http://www .pantsuitpoliticsshow.com/show-archives/ 2016/9/19/season-2-episode-15-the-great -redhead-debate.

7. Byron Katie, quoted in Martha Beck, "The Three Questions You Need to Ask Yourself Before Criticizing Someone," Oprah.com, accessed June 21, 2018, http://www.oprah.com/inspiration/martha -beck-how-to-stop-criticizing-everyone.

Chapter 6: Get Curious

1. Steve Liesman, "What's in a Name? Lots When It Comes to Obamacare/ACA," CNBC, September 26, 2013, https://www .cnbc.com/2013/09/26/whats-in-a-name -lots-when-it-comes-to-obamacareaca .html.

2. Maane Khatchatourian, "Jimmy Kimmel: Americans Don't Know Difference Be-

tween Obamacare, Affordable Care Act," *Variety,* October 1, 2013, http://variety.com/2013/tv/news/jimmy-kimmel-americans-dont-know-difference-between-obamacare-affordable-care-act-1200685381/.

3. The UN Security Council's five permanent members — China, France, Russia, the United Kingdom, the United States — plus Germany.

4. James Taranto, "The Politicization of Motherhood," *Wall Street Journal,* October 27, 2017, https://www.wsj.com/articles/the-politicization-of-motherhood-1509144044.

5. "Democrat National Convention: Part I," *Pantsuit Politics,* July 27, 2016, http://www.pantsuitpoliticsshow.com/show-archives/2016/7/27/democrat-national-convention-part-i?rq=dnc.

Chapter 7: Embrace the Paradox

1. Jeffrey M. Jones, "Americans' Identification as Independents Back Up in 2017," Gallup, January 8, 2018, http://news.gallup.com/poll/225056/americans-identification-independents-back-2017.aspx.

2. "Jon Stewart's America," *Crossfire,*

CNN.com, October 15, 2004, http://
transcripts.cnn.com/TRANSCRIPTS/
0410/15/cf.01.html.

3. Paul Begala, "Begala: The Day Jon Stewart Blew Up My Show," CNN, February
12, 2015, https://www.cnn.com/2015/02/
12/opinion/begala-stewart-blew-up
-crossfire/index.html.

4. Richard Rohr, *A New Way of Seeing . . . A
New Way of Being: Jesus and Paul,* Center
for Action and Contemplation, 2007,
audio CD.

5. Krista Tippett, *Einstein's God: Conversations About Science and the Human Spirit*
(New York: Penguin Books, 2010), 7.

6. "The Briefcase: Dr. Tamara Tweel on
Involuntary Miscarriages and Voluntary
Abortions," *Pantsuit Politics,* February 3,
2017, http://www.pantsuitpoliticsshow
.com/show-archives/2017/2/2/season-3
-episode-4-dr-tamara-tweel.

7. Tamara Mann, "Heartbeat: My Involuntary Miscarriage and 'Voluntary Abortion'
in Ohio," *The Blog,* Huff Post, November
1, 2012, https://www.huffingtonpost.com/
tamara-mann/heartbeat-involuntary
-miscarriage-and-voluntary-abortion-in
-ohio_b_2050888.html.

8. Mann.

9. "The Briefcase" episode.

10. "The Briefcase" episode.

Chapter 8: Get Comfortable with Being Uncomfortable

1. Nick DiUlio, "More Than Half of American Adults Don't Have a Will," Fox Business, February 6, 2017, https://www.foxbusiness.com/features/2017/02/06/more-than-half-american-adults-dont-have-will.html.
2. Sherry Pagoto, "The Real Reason We Don't Exercise," *Psychology Today,* November 10, 2014, https://www.psychologytoday.com/blog/shrink/201411/the-real-reason-we-dont-exercise.
3. Pema Chödrön, "Pema Chödrön 'Dunzie',"YouTube video, 2:02, posted by Omega Institute for Holistic Studies, September 1, 2009, https://www.youtube.com/watch?v=p7kFvETUT3s.
4. Amanda Petrusich, " 'American Vandal' and Our Search for Meaning," *The New Yorker,* January 1, 2018, https://www.newyorker.com/magazine/2018/01/01/american-vandal-and-our-search-for-meaning.
5. Katherine Freund et al., "Hospice Eligibility in Patients Who Died in a Tertiary Care Center," *Journal of Hospital Medicine*

7, no. 3 (March 2012): 218–23, https://www.journalofhospitalmedicine.com/jhospmed/article/127524/hospice-eligibility.

6. [Format of communication (Facebook direct message, email message, etc.)] to authors, [Date].

7. Kathryn Casteel, "There Is More Than One Opioid Crisis," FiveThirtyEight, January 17, 2018, https://fivethirtyeight.com/features/there-is-more-than-one-opioid-crisis/.

8. Casteel. It's likely that we don't have accurate information because of the way that such deaths are reported. The numbers could be even higher.

9. Jesse Mechanic, "When a Drug Epidemic Hit White America, Addiction Became a Disease," Huffington Post, July 10, 2017, https://www.huffingtonpost.com/entry/when-a-drug-epidemic-hit-white-america-addiction-became_us_5963a588e4b08f5c97d06b9a.

10. Tom McKee, "Narcan Debate: Saves Lives or Enables Addicts?" WCPO Cincinnati, August 27, 2016, https://www.wcpo.com/news/local-news/kenton-county/narcan-debate-save-lives-or-enables-addicts.

11. "Opioid Overdose: Prescribing Data,"

Centers for Disease Control and Prevention, last updated August 30, 2017, https://www.cdc.gov/drugoverdose/data/prescribing.html.

12. "The Role of Pharmaceutical Companies in the Opioid Epidemic," Addictions .com, accessed May 12, 2018, https://www.addictions.com/opiate/the-role-of-pharmaceutical-companies-in-the-opioid-epidemic/.

13. Douglas C. McDonald, Kenneth Carlson, David Izrael, "Geographic Variation in Opioid Prescribing in the U.S.," *Journal of Pain* 13, no. 10 (October 2012): 988–96, https://doi.org/10.1016/j.jpain.2012.07.007.

14. Sarah Kliff, " 'We Started It': Atul Gawande on Doctors' Role in the Opioid Epidemic," Vox, September 8, 2017, https://www.vox.com/2017/9/8/16270370/atul-gawande-opioid-weeds.

15. "Opioid Overdose: Prescription Opioid Data," Centers for Disease Control and Prevention.

16. Leonid Bershidsky, "Supply, Not Despair, Caused the Opioid Epidemic," Bloomberg Opinion, January 10, 2018, https://www.bloomberg.com/view/articles/2018-01-10/supply-not-despair-caused-the-opioid-epidemic.

17. Rebecca L. Haffajee and Michelle M. Mello, "Drug Companies' Liability for the Opioid Epidemic," *New England Journal of Medicine* 377 (2017): 2301–2305, https://doi.org/10.1056/NEJMp1710756.

18. "Doctors & Medical Industry Complicit in Opioid Epidemic?" Northeast Addictions Treatment Center, December 6, 2017, https://neaddictions.com/doctors-medical-industry-complicit-opioid-epidemic/.

19. Adam Grant, "Kids, Would You Please Start Fighting?" *New York Times,* November 4, 2017, https://www.nytimes.com/2017/11/04/opinion/sunday/kids-would-you-please-start-fighting.html.

20. Tara Brach, "Tara Talks — What Are You Unwilling to Feel?" YouTube video, 2:42, posted by Tara Brach, May 2, 2017, https://www.youtube.com/watch?v=LhzLZjp2QpQ.

21. Harold S. Kushner, *When Bad Things Happen to Good People* (1981; New York: Schocken Books, 2001), 180.

22. "P.S. About the First Amendment," *Pantsuit Politics,* August 17, 2017, http://www.pantsuitpoliticsshow.com/new-blog/2017/8/17/ps-about-the-first-amendment.

23. Quoted in Bill Moyers's remarks at Coffin's funeral, transcript at "Remembering

Bill Coffin: Bill Moyers," PBS, April 20,
2006, http://www.pbs.org/wnet/religion
andethics/2006/04/20/april-20–2006
-remembering-bill-coffin-bill-moyers/
2954/.

Chapter 9: Exit the Echo Chamber

1. Reuters, "Most American Adults Get
News from Social Media," *Fortune,* September 8, 2017, http://fortune.com/2017/
09/08/facebook-twitter-snap-news/.
2. Email to authors, November 30, 2016.
3. Letter used with permission.
4. Email to authors, January 25, 2018.

Chapter 10: Keep It Nuanced

1. JTowne, "Godmother of a New Genre?"
review of *Pantsuit Politics* podcast, March
4, 2016, iTunes.
2. *Saturday Night Live,* "Dinner Discussion,"
featuring Heidi Gardner, Will Ferrell,
Beck Bennett, Kate McKinnon, Aidy
Bryant, and Kenan Thompson, aired January 27, 2018, on NBC, available online as
YouTube video, 4:25, https://www.youtube
.com/watch?v=evWiz6WRbCA.
3. Katie Way, "I Went on a Date with Aziz
Ansari. It Turned into the Worst Night of

My Life," babe.net, January 13, 2018, https://babe.net/2018/01/13/aziz-ansari -28355.

4. Jasmine Andersson, "The Allegations Against Aziz Ansari Should Not Surprise Us — Just Because Men Call Themselves Feminists It Doesn't Mean They Are," Independent, January 14, 2018, https:// www.independent.co.uk/voices/aziz-ansari -master-of-none-sexual-misconduct -allegations-feminism-a8158886.html.

5. Caitlin Flanagan, "The Humiliation of Aziz Ansari," The Atlantic, January 14, 2018, https://www.theatlantic.com/ entertainment/archive/2018/01/the -humiliation-of-aziz-ansari/550541/.

6. Steffanee Wang, "Aziz Ansari Accused of 'Sexual Assault' by a Brooklyn Photographer," Fader, January 14, 2018, http:// www.thefader.com/2018/01/14/aziz-ansari -sexual-assault-accusation.

ABOUT THE AUTHORS

Sarah Stewart Holland has always had a passion for talking politics. As the creator and cohost of the hit bipartisan political podcast *Pantsuit Politics*, she has turned that passion into a career. When she's not opining about policy or the latest political firestorm from behind the mic, Sarah is raising her three young sons with her husband in her hometown of Paducah, Kentucky, where she served on the Paducah City Commission.

Before turning to the mic, Sarah wrote about parenting and politics on her blog *Bluegrass Redhead.* Her writing has also been published on the *Atlantic, Huffington Post, Scary Mommy,* and *BlogHer.* Sarah received her BA from Transylvania University, and her JD from American University's Washington College of Law in Washington, DC.

Beth Silvers is a wife, mother, recovering lawyer, and business coach. She lives in Union, Kentucky, with her husband, Chad; daughters, Jane and Ellen; and miniature schnauzer, Lucy. Beth received her JD from the University of Kentucky College of Law, then began her career in the Cincinnati office of Taft Stettinius and Hollister LLP as an associate. She worked in the firm's restructuring group for almost six years before shifting her focus to human resources, diversity, and operations. When *Pantsuit Politics* and *The Nuanced Life* podcasts outgrew their status as hobbies, she left the firm and opened her coaching practice. Beth has been named a Human Resources Game Changer by *WorkForce Magazine,* one of Cincinnati's "40 Under 40" business leaders, and one of Ohio's Most Powerful and Influential Women by the Ohio Diversity Council. Beth is a ministry partner of Florence Christian Church (Disciples of Christ), a graduate of Leadership Northern Kentucky, and member of the Ohio Justice and Policy Center board of directors. She loves people, politics, poetry, and watermelon.

The employees of Thorndike Press hope you have enjoyed this Large Print book. All our Thorndike, Wheeler, and Kennebec Large Print titles are designed for easy reading, and all our books are made to last. Other Thorndike Press Large Print books are available at your library, through selected bookstores, or directly from us.

For information about titles, please call:
(800) 223-1244

or visit our website at:
gale.com/thorndike

To share your comments, please write:
Publisher
Thorndike Press
10 Water St., Suite 310
Waterville, ME 04901